# A Divine Appointments...

Melissa Giomi

Melissa Giomi
Facebook: @MelissaGiomiauthor
Instagram: @melissa.giomi

First Paperback Edition September 2023

ISBN 979-8-218-26459-8 (paperback)
ISBN 979-8-218-26460-4 (ebook)

Library of Congress Control Number: 2023915776

Edited by Pia Edberg, piaedberg.com
Blurb by Book Blurb Magic, IG: @bookblurbmagic
Cover & interior design by Karolina Wudniak, karolinawudniak.com

# A Divine
# Appointments...

From His heart, to my pen...

# Table of Contents

# ...the Greatest Gift

# ...with the Father

# Introduction

I'm delighted that you picked up *Divine Appointments...* the companion to my first book, *Divine Encounters...* the culmination of over ten years of writing.

Both books give me the opportunity to share the healing and beautiful things I have experienced on my journey with Jesus, and I am eternally grateful for it.

There have been lovely, exciting, joy-filled times interspersed with sadness, fear, and a long battle with breast cancer. I discovered there was always hope and the Divine is all around us, as close as our next breath.

Beauty and joy can be found in an ordinary day. There is peace and restoration in the ancient rhythms of nature and deep healing in the chaos of this life we have been given. Divine appointments are being offered to us constantly if we pause to watch, listen, and accept the Creator's invitation to talk with Him.

My hope is that as you journey with me, you will find exactly what you need and be richly blessed. Peace be with you and thank you for reading my book.

# ...Living with Hope

# Blessed

My COFFEE MUG has the word Blessed inscribed across the front. The letters are big and bold, like a confident declaration.

Sitting at my kitchen table, I watch the morning unfold in my garden. There are a variety of birds at the feeders that sing as they jostle for position. They wait their turn, sometimes with nice attitudes and other times, not. Other birds scratch and scritch among the garden debris, ferreting out whatever treasures are hidden in the rich dirt. Watching these birds go about their daily business, I think about the word blessed. The dictionary says it means consecrated; holy; sacred; blissfully happy, or contented. These words are beautiful. I want to be these words, to feel and live in these words.

Living and being blessed often seem elusive, like a thought or elevated idea that is difficult to truly capture. As I pondered this idea, I began to see that the word blessed is not a higher thought on a difficult-to-achieve spiritual plane.

Imagine a typical day—you wake up and grab some coffee in your favorite mug. Perhaps you watch the morning unfold on the patio as a soft breeze floats past, all kinds of sounds and scents in the air. What if you decided to be grateful that you are alive, able to see, smell, and experience nature going about its business in the Divine order of things? Is that not sacred, bringing bliss and contentment?

What if you witness a startling and unusual act of kindness causing you to pause, tear up and have your faith in humanity restored, if even for a moment? Is that not holy? Is that intersection of the Divine and the human not sacred ground? I wonder, when I'm making dinner, listening to music, or chatting with Jesus on a walk in my neighborhood, if those places become sacred, holy, and divine. Blessed.

But…what if the day isn't full of things that make me blissfully happy? The car accident that totals the car, the child who makes a poor choice, and you see no clear way out. Maybe cruel words were hurled in the heat of the moment, and they can't be taken back. Perhaps there is a diagnosis you never saw coming. Is there room here to declare, "I am blessed?" Yes.

Some blessings come after the hurt and wounds. The Divine often shows up in miraculous ways, turning devastation into glory, failure into victory, wounding into strength, and the impossible into something to be remembered in awe and reverence because there seemed to be no good ending, yet there was.

To live blessed, we need to be alert and seek it out. It won't always show up immediately. Blessings may not be dressed up in blissful happiness and a cute outfit. Blessings may come dirty, scuffed up, straggling, and a bit off-kilter, but they will come. I have seen them come in both forms—equally holy, sacred, and consecrated. Blessed.

I want to live with an extravagant hope expecting blessing. I want to bloom where I am planted and thrive, no matter what it looks like. Holy, divine, sacred, and blissful happiness is all around, waiting with open arms for us to slow down and seek it. What is sought will be found.

# Let There Be

GENESIS 1:3 "And God said, 'Let there be light,' and there was light."

This short statement in Genesis 1:3 called the world into existence. The Spirit of God hovered over the empty, formless mass of Earth, declaring it to exist out of nothing.

In my mind, I see it—deep blackness empty of hope and life, the vast absolute silence of it all. Nothingness. It's overwhelming to think about because we have never experienced absolute nothingness, the absence of all sound. How would that feel? Suffocating? Terrifying? Absolutely alone. Pinpricks of goose bumps form as I picture what the Creator hovered over in that place devoid of everything.

But He said, "Let there be…"

That is not a wish or a casual comment. "Let there be." It's a command. As the Spirit of God hovered, He already knew what He was going to call into existence. He always knew and dedicated a specific time and place for it to happen.

Omnipotent. Omniscient. Omnipresent. Alpha and Omega. The power, compassion, patience, wisdom, authority, and mystery wrapped up in these words is nothing short of awe-inspiring. It is humbling and breathtaking. Everything becoming as He intended by the words of His mouth—nothing accidental or happenstance. "So is my word that goes out from my mouth: It will not return to me empty but will accomplish what I desire and achieve the purpose for which I sent it."[1]

This word from His mouth included you and me.

As the earth we inhabit was being called into existence, you and I were on His mind. When there was nothing but blackness and silence, we were thought of and intimately known down to the minute cellular details of our being. The exact timing of our birth, our parents, our siblings, our friends, and our entire sphere of existence was known, decided, and waiting for His word to release us to be and do what He ordained from the very beginning. I imagine the joy and excitement in the heavenlies as each of us was sent forth!

It is hard to know what to do with the knowledge that we have always been known, cherished, and so very loved; that before we existed in a worldly way, the exact number of hairs on our heads was decided, the color of our eyes was chosen, and the path we were created to walk was purposely plotted out. There is no surprise or plot twist for Him. Our journey may be twisty, tedious, and full of the unexpected, unwanted, and unexplained to our limited wisdom, but not to the One who set it all in motion with the command, "Let there be…"

---

1   Isaiah 55:11

I wonder how many times each day He declares over us, "Let there be" …a job, provision, healing, restoration, a safe trip, a friend, an angelic intervention, hope, and protection from evil. His words never return void, and they achieve all that He sends them forth to accomplish. He's declaring it over you right now. "Let there be" …hope, peace, blessings, and victory! You are safe, you are known, you are of immense value.

# Lessons from Cancer

OVER TEN YEARS AGO, I was diagnosed with aggressive, fast--moving breast cancer. I immediately began an exhausting and terrifying set of surgeries and treatments. Our lives were upended, exposed, and thrust into a trajectory of the unknown for over two years. During this trial, I learned so much about myself, the resilience of the human body, the primal urge to survive, and that in my frailty and weakness, I am made strong.

On April 26, 2012, at 2:15 pm, I was told, "You are cancer free!"

Each year as the day approaches, many things run through my mind. The random memories of the cancer center and its "one of a kind, not found anywhere else" smell, the peppermint candies I sucked on to try to mask the terrible taste of saline and chemo, the ice chips I held in my mouth to keep painful ulcers from forming (I cannot stand ice in my drinks or mouth to this day), the blanket I brought to keep warm during treatments and comfy pink slipper socks. I still hear the sound of radiation equipment being dialed into place with strange and other-worldly whirs, clicks, and bleeps. It was lonely in the brightly lit, freezing radiation room as the technicians went behind thick layers of protective safety walls, and I lay there exposed, cold, and numb, willing the machine noises to stop, praying I wouldn't burn.

I have treasured memories of my husband going with me to each treatment and my dearest friends praying and chatting with me when I needed them. The distraction of good company meant so much to me, even though it was hard and uncomfortable for them.

The beautiful memories of my little second-grade boy asking me to hop in his bed as he tucked me in with blankets and got out his books to read to me and tell me jokes. Blessed. Loved. Precious. This sweet boy is now a brave, courageous young man in the United States Army—respectful, strong, and determined with a kind and compassionate heart.

It meant the world to me when my sweet sixth-grade girl would tell me about her day with the ups and downs of middle school; feeling so blessed that she shared with me and praying so hard that I would have years ahead of me to listen to her talk. She is an adult now—a beautiful, compassionate, strong, and amazing young woman with a kind and generous heart. God answered that prayer for more time with my family.

My body fought to beat this invader named breast cancer, enduring extreme treatments, pain, panic, nausea, steroids, exhaustion, and hair loss but never stopped fighting. God gave me strength to make it through one more day, one more test, and one more treatment. He did it. He is absolutely faithful. His eyes never left me, and His tears mixed with my own as I was wrapped in His arms, crying out my fear, rage, and frustration—wondering if I would die.

I am still learning to view my body through a different filter. I am proud of my scars. They shout out that a battle was waged and won. I want to enjoy every second of life I am given, so sometimes I choose to eat dessert and not worry about how I will look in a swimsuit. I am alive, and that is enough.

Despite days of sadness, fear of the unknown, rage, pain, and brain fog, I told myself I would get through this—that cancer would not win. God absolutely gave me more than I could handle because we were never meant to live this life in our own strength. I chose to believe God would be with me through every test, treatment, and every bit of good and bad news. I held on to that, and He proved Himself faithful, merciful, and compassionate. Yes, it was the hardest thing I have ever done. Yes, it put my body, mind, and soul to the ultimate test. I am an overcomer, and so are you.

When other trials come along, like trials always do, I remind myself to look back at all that God brought me through. As an Army Mom, I feel overwhelmed at times and draw on past fortitude, peace, strength, and flexibility to navigate this new season of life. I battled cancer and won; I can do hard things because He gave me a warrior heart and soul.

Life is hard, unpredictable, and unfair, but if you look closely, you can find nuggets of joy and hidden treasures of beauty in everything. It is there waiting to be discovered, but you must change your filter from a victim mentality and choose life—choose to seek peace, hope, and sweetness in whatever is swirling around you. I promise you it IS there. I remind myself daily that I CAN do all things through Christ who strengthens me. You can, too. It is His breath in my lungs. He saved my life, and I am thankful for another day to live out whatever He has planned for me.

My hope as I travel through this next chapter of life is that I leave everyone better than I found them—that encouragement, compassion, and hope will trail behind me like a gentle beacon defying the darkness and shining the light of the One who is Light.

"But I'll take the hand of those who don't know the way, who can't see where they're going. I'll be a personal guide to them, directing them through unknown country. I'll be right there to show them what roads to take to make sure they don't fall into the ditch. These are the things I'll be doing for them—sticking with them, not leaving them for a minute." Isaiah 42:16

"The light shines in the darkness, and the darkness has not overcome it." John 1:5

# Hope Grove

HE IS UP before the sun rises. His camo-colored backpack lies on the backseat of the old, dark blue Jeep. It's full of water bottles, snacks, a sketch pad, and sunscreen. A few haphazard beach towels and a trusty old blanket are tossed on the floor. The smell of his hastily grabbed cappuccino wafts and swirls around him; it's a comforting scent and tastes like liquid gold.

He enjoys road trips, especially heading to the forested mountains of the Sierras. He gets an early start to avoid traffic and people. The many laned freeways of suburbia inch down into two-laned, curvy mountain roads. Gentle hills give way to foothills dotted with trees and brush. Soon he will be in the mountains. The anticipation in his bones is invigorating!

As the Jeep climbs up and up, twisting and turning on the winding road, he feels some of the tension leave him. His shoulders drop a little. The tightness around his ears and neck loosen up. He has been full of knots, worry, and vague feelings of frustration.

It won't be long now. The turnoff is coming soon. He feels the pull and tug on his heart and body that this mountain trail always conjures up in his soul.

Turning the signal on, he eases into the small, wooded parking lot. It's empty. Yes! He doesn't want distractions today. He needs to be alone to refresh and get some perspective. Such unsettled emotions plague him lately. They bubble up and, at times, consume him. How does he get out of this slump? Nothing is going as planned. His big interview was a disaster. He was completely unprepared, and the failure of it still reddens his face with embarrassment. High expectations and dashed dreams camp out in his mind. Others in his sphere are successful and fast-moving. They are further along than he is, and it rubs, scrapes, and gnaws at his thoughts.

Yet…another feeling has been hanging out in his mind, as well—a rushing sensation that pulses along in his very blood. It's not unpleasant but unusual. He can't quite put his finger on it. Deep down, he knows that whatever it is, it's calling him, telling him it is time to get to the mountains.

Well, here he is in the mountains…

He takes in the stillness punctuated by calling birds, rustling trees, and the beautiful, blessed silence of the forest. He belongs here. This is his place. He feels known and accepted by the mountain, the trees, and the scent of warming pine that he loves so much. He takes deep, deep breaths to capture the scent in his lungs and hold on to the scent memory.

Hefting his backpack from the Jeep, he grabs a beach towel. He plans to find a quiet place to sit and become one with the earth and forest. Maybe he will break out the sketch pad. Downing the remaining cappuccino, he is off to the trail and whatever adventure awaits him.

He chooses a brisk but easy pace. He likes to feel his blood pumping but doesn't want to miss a single thing the forest will show him this morning. It's been a while since he's hiked here, and he wonders if it's changed. He soaks up all the mountain offers him, sounds only found in the forest—creatures scurrying and fussing in the undergrowth vying for bugs and seeds; loud jays that scold and screech shouting the forest gossip; louder, more defined thumps and rustles that come from something bigger.

All these are music to his ears and a feast for his eyes. Moving gingerly along the path, he notices some random bursts of white hidden among the detritus on the forest floor, snagging along the bark of some trees and bushes. Hmm. Odd. In all his years spent hiking these forest paths, he doesn't remember this strange white stuff. He stops and waits a moment along a curved spot in the trail. He looks back and sees that the placement of the white doesn't seem quite as random as he thought. Was it placed here purposely? The urgent feeling of beckoning and calling is coursing through his blood again. Interesting. "What is this?" he wonders aloud.

He moves on, alert this time for more white. He spies it snared on a fallen pine tree and heads over for a closer look. It appears to be feathery and light, a bit silky, airy, and so soft. As he runs this white, airy softness between his fingers, a peaceful feeling of safety and rest settle over him.

Not knowing what to make of this, he searches the path in

front of him and spies more white as the trail twists and turns out of sight. Senses piqued, he travels along this mysterious path that enchants him.

Rounding a bend, he spots a small, weather-beaten sign. It sits on a dilapidated post covered with moss and lichen. Tiny yellow flowers surround the crooked base. The sign says Hope Grove with a faded red arrow pointing off to the right. The white, airy material is profuse here at the right-hand fork. He doesn't remember any of this; is he lost? Oddly, he doesn't have that frightened, adrenaline rush feeling of being lost. Instead, he feels found.

He doesn't hesitate as he follows the fork to the right toward Hope Grove. He feels anticipation and, is that joy? It might be…

There is a small tunnel-like area up ahead where smaller trees and creeping vines, snagged with the white feathery material, make a covered spot over the trail. He moves through and emerges into a pine grove. There is a small area of meadow grasses and wildflowers dipping in the breeze. Fascinating! He moves about this little grove stopping to look closely at the flowers, sturdy grasses, and the light; the beautiful, soft light.

Excited, he finds the perfect spot to toss down the beach towel. His mind is clear and uncluttered. He enjoys the sounds, scents, and beauty. It refreshes him. It is actively restoring him. He feels it; he knows it. His soul and spirit unclench, and he decides to let it all go. Peace. Safety. Rest.

After allowing his tired body and battered spirit to breathe again, he opens his backpack, grabs snacks and water, and looks at the sketch pad lying there. It wills him to open it, to capture and fill the pages with what the grove speaks to him.

Taking in the entirety of the meadow and grove, he sees a well-worn sign to his left. Hope Grove. The words are written in faded blue letters. Floating off one corner of this aged sign, he sees the white again. The way the light hits it, the way it flutters and moves with the gauzy breeze, looks like feathers—white, airy, wispy feathers. Happy and joyful, they call to him. He is not alone here in Hope Grove. The presence is not sinister; it is a Spirit of joy, belonging, and peace. It is sacred and intimate. Here he is wanted. There are no expectations placed on him. He is enough. The fear that sticks to him of late falls away, and in its place is confidence.

Opening the sketchbook, he surprises himself at how deftly he captures the light and beauty of this place. The way it falls between the pine trees in stark but gentle beams. The sign is dappled by the rays that penetrate its corner of the grove, illuminating the white feathers in a mysterious, forest-y, and peaceful way.

In between his drawing and snacking, he allows the peace and silence of this grove to seep into his spirit and his bones. He will not forget.

The light and sounds of the forest shift to early evening. It's time to go. Feeling wistful as he packs up his things, he is careful to leave this magical place undisturbed. He will leave behind the fear, defeat, and crippling expectations, and he will take hope, confidence, and peace with him.

# Taking up Space

FOR SOME OF US, when we hear the phrase "taking up space," it can send out a negative vibe. It speaks to being too much, unnecessary, and in the way. It calls up feelings of being unwanted and blocking or taking away from someone or something else of more value and importance—of the need to be silent and unseen.

How many of us go about our days feeling like we take up space? I have and sometimes still do. It is as if the air we breathe is meant for someone else, and our presence is a nuisance. It is dismissive and lonely.

So, what if we turned the narrative around and thought of taking up space as a positive and important part of living, the very thing we were created to do?

I love how God has woven unconditional love, hope, and purpose into His narrative about each of us. It isn't selfish or arrogant to believe what our Creator says about us. It is hard to live in this world, and He knows that. He knows what it's like to be us because He lived among us in a physical body with all the good and bad that goes along with that. Fully man and fully God. He knows how rejection, cruel words, dismissive attitudes, and being hated feels. He understands the way it wounds and taints everything when you are made to feel that the physical space you occupy is wasted and not accepted, as if you have no voice and will never be heard.

These scriptures are a beautiful example of how important we are and how much the world needs us to take up space.

Luke 12:7 "And the very hairs on your head are all numbered. So don't be afraid; you are more valuable to God than a whole flock of sparrows."

Joshua 1:9 "This is my command—be strong and courageous! Do not be afraid or discouraged. For the LORD your God is with you wherever you go."

Isaiah 46:4 "I will be your God throughout your lifetime—until your hair is white with age. I made you, and I will care for you. I will carry you along and save you."

Do you see how treasured and valuable you are? You were created to fill a very specific and special place in this world, to use your voice. God commands us to be strong and have courage! He promises to never leave us, to carry us and care for us. We will never be snatched away, shushed, pushed to the back, ignored, or minimized in His sight. We are seen, known, and deeply loved.

We must find the courage to take up space and no longer apologize for our voice, our strength, and our calling. By using our voices to empower, encourage and call out the beauty and value we see in others, we leave a beautiful legacy of hope in our wake. Imagine what might happen when we sing the song that He placed in our spirits to bless those in the spaces around us. Take up the space that you were created to hold. You are exactly where you need to be in the beautiful tapestry He is weaving as our lives intersect and intertwine in a divine dance—all of His children moving in time and rhythm to the music of Heaven.

# Choose Hope

1 PETER 1:6-9 "So be truly glad! There is wonderful joy ahead, even though it is necessary for you to endure many trials for a while. These trials are only to test your faith, to show that it is strong and pure. It is being tested as fire tests and purifies gold—and your faith is far more precious to God than mere gold. So if your faith remains strong after being tried by fiery trials, it will bring you much praise and glory, and honor on the day when Jesus Christ is revealed to the whole world. You love him even though you have never seen him. Though you do not see him, you trust him; and even now, you are happy with a glorious, inexpressible joy. Your reward for trusting him will be the salvation of your souls."

These are hard words to read during a painful trial that seems to have no end. It blindsides us, and we reel with feeling overwhelmed, unprepared, and out of control. Maybe this trial was caused by the result of someone else's choices that we didn't see coming. Maybe it stems from our own bad decisions, and we are left stumbling through consequences that we brought to our doorstep. We have all been there at least once, and it hurts. It is confusing and frightening. It feels like there is no way out from under the damage. We feel helpless. How desperately we want Jesus to take it all away!

The thing I have learned about trials is oftentimes, God uses them to change us. When we are living unchallenged, complacent, comfortable, and self-reliant, He may use a tough situation to move us away from destructive patterns and steer us in a new direction.

After a breast cancer diagnosis, my world collapsed in a matter of moments. Nothing made sense. No one could walk this path for me or take it away, and there was no one, but God, who could carry me through this. I had a choice to make at that moment; allow despair and terror to reign in my world, or choose to put it at His feet, extravagantly hope, and believe there was a purpose somewhere in this. I chose hope, and it was my lifeline. I discovered that feeling helpless is NOT the same as being helpless. God is always as close as our next breath and never leaves us to face trials alone.

I truly believe He uses our pain and rough seasons to purify and beautify us and our faith so that one day He will clearly see His image in us. Self-reliance, pride, and self-righteousness have no place amid a life-altering trial. It is surprising and beautiful how compassion and empathy are born during difficulty, pain, and loss if we choose to trust ourselves to the One who created us.

He will make a way. We can be confident that God will separate something priceless from the dross of our experiences.

Imagine God's joy and delight as He skims off the gunk and sees HIS image in us! I hope it makes you smile knowing the Creator of galaxies is so invested and in love with each one of us that He takes all the time necessary to allow us to feel the heat of trials so that He can one day bring forth for the world to see, the radiant beauty of our life testimonies. We can be a beacon of salvation, and love to a world full of hurting humans who need to hear a word of hope and see a life redeemed.

# Hometown

THERE ARE only a few more miles to go until her exit. The familiarity of these bends and curves in the highway prick at her mind. In a comforting way, it feels like a buttery old glove made of soft leather molded to your hand. It fits snugly and securely, wrapping you in warmth and a thin layer of protection. However, if she's being honest, she isn't feeling very secure. How many years has it been since she's been "home"? Her nerves are a bit jangly and wiry, and she wonders about her decision to visit her hometown. Will it fill the void gnawing at her heart—that unsettled feeling of something unfinished and dangling, something needing her attention to bring closure and perhaps much-needed peace? What is it that needs her to let go?

Sipping the last dregs of her Peets oat milk, light foam latte, Natalie rounds the last bend. Here is the slight rise in the highway with the old barn in the field to the left. It once was a rusty red, but with all the weathering it's endured, the color is now a dusty brown. The big sign hangs by a tilted chain over the arched entrance. The country lane leading up to it still has potholes and ruts. The name painted on the sign is kind of hard to read, but Natalie knows it by heart—Whispering Oaks Farm. The small orchard to the right is still standing, but the trees have aged, gnarled, and twisted.

Two dappled horses languidly munch grass hay in their tidy corral. Natalie remembers Mr. Jameson allowing her and her friends to bring apples and carrots to his horses. She loved the feel of their chin whiskers tickling the palm of her hand and the intelligence in their dark eyes.

Her exit is next. She signals and slows to follow it down and to the right. There's a stoplight now where there once was a STOP sign. At the green light, she heads into town.

So much looks the same. There are tweaks, updated signs, and fresh paint on some of the storefronts, but most of the businesses look the same as when she left. Almost imperceptibly, her grip on the steering wheel loosens. Her neck and shoulders drop as muscles unclench and settle a bit. Something is comforting here in the old and familiar.

Parking along the street bordering the town square, Natalie steps out and stretches, watching people entering the bookstore and the new-to-her café on the opposite side of the square. People stroll around the grassy, tree-lined park, some with coffee in green cups from the café. Others carry restless children demanding to get down to run, screech, and play in the small, shady play area. Still, others sit and watch the world go by or read their books.

Natalie walks the park, taking in the scent of the pine trees growing in a cluster at one end. Pine has always held an old, safe, happy scent. The splashing fountain is updated and much cleaner now, cheerful in its bubbling and chuckling. She feels the corners of her mouth turn up and can't help smiling at the happy fountain. She remembers picnics and cold sodas in the summer on the grass right here in this spot.

She sits for a bit to take it all in. She did have happy times here. She did... How long will she allow that one memory, with its wounds and startling betrayal, to stifle her? Natalie was sure that moving away would force that memory to fade into the jumble of her fast-paced new life in a bigger city with more people and chaos to drown it out. Maybe it did for a little while. Is this why she feels such a draw and pull on her heart to be back here? Is it time to let that hurtful memory go?

She has such a need for some peace and joy, some happy contentment without the roiling bitterness flooding it all out. Yes. She thinks nostalgia and healing are what's been calling to her...

Waking up before the alarm clock, Dominic feels a push to get moving this morning. It's an interesting anticipation, and he wonders what it wants from him.

With his morning routine complete, Dominic grabs his keys, wallet, and phone and scoots out the door. On the way to the café, he remembers he needs oat milk. He stops at the neighborhood market to grab some and notices a flat of bright-colored lollipops by the cash register. For some reason, they catch his eye. Hmmm. These could be a fun addition to the pick-up counter. Dominic buys the flat, picturing the short, wide-mouthed vase he will put these lollies in as a catchy display. His long-time barista,

Meredith, will roll her eyes and tease him for it. He chuckles as he figures out some brilliant comebacks to her good-natured ribbing.

Opening his shop, The Cuppa Café, Dominic gives it a once over like he does every morning. He turns the hand-painted OPEN sign facing out. "I wonder who will stop by today?" he asks the pastry display.

The church that her grandma brought her to as a kid is down the street, about two blocks from the town square. Natalie remembers the smell of wax, leather-bound hymnals, and a faint, flowery scent. She reaches the steps of the church and takes it in for a few minutes before trying the big double doors. It looks the same, radiating a welcoming sense of belonging. The white paint by the doors is scuffed and peeling in a few places along the sides and near the stained-glass window. The church spire points up, up, up.

Her breathing feels easier and lighter, not so strained and constricted. Funny, she never noticed how hard it's been lately to breathe deeply. Feeling a calm, lovely serenity beckoning her, Natalie steps into the chapel. The memories hit her, enveloping and wrapping around her like an old quilt. Safety. Comfort. Peace. The frenetic energy drains away as she sits on a faded, padded pew and rests. She rests mind and body, allowing her spirit to drink in the memories that pour forth. Healing memories. Church potlucks, kids' choir, Christmas Eve services, and VBS—where the teachers always had a supply of sweet, bright-colored lollipops as prizes. Such happy times!

Delicious feelings and gentle memories smooth out the worn, cracked, bandaged-up places in her heart; even the place where the wounds and betrayal are hidden is tended to with mercy, grace, and healing. It's time to let go. As Natalie lifts her head, she notices dust motes floating above her, dancing and moving toward the beautiful stained-glass window. She imagines those motes as tiny balloons with wispy tails carrying the wounds and pain, ascending toward the gentle light to be kept and tended by Someone else now. Freedom. Joy. Nostalgia. And hope, blessed hope.

Her time in the church brings restoration and lightness. Nostalgia is healing. Old things and memories hold a special balm that soothes and brings clarity and peace. There was a reckoning in her spirit that needed to happen, and it did.

Warm, soothing coffee sounds lovely right now, so Natalie makes her way to The Cuppa Café. Pushing open the doors, the bright, welcoming scent of coffee brushes up against her. A man in a green apron is adding scones to his pastry display. "Hi, and welcome in!" he calls.

The barista named Meredith finishes rinsing some cups and hurries over to take her order of a large oat milk latte. "Hey, you're in luck! I grabbed a carton of oat milk on my way in this morning," Dominic tells her. Natalie smiles as she waits for Meredith to make her drink, crafting a design in the frothy foam.

Walking to the end of the coffee bar, bright colors in a short, wide-mouthed vase catch her eye. There is a sign propped up against the vase "Take One." Oh my...the lollipops. What in the world? Natalie carefully picks a bright yellow one.

"Here you go!" Meredith hands her the cup and turns to start on the next order. Heading to a nearby table, Natalie sits and looks in the cup. The carefully crafted foam design is a balloon with a wispy tail. Her eyes mist. The balloon and yellow lollipop blur a bit. The way this entire day blended in a perfect symphony of comforting nostalgia, healing release, and budding joy touches her heart and soul in a way she has never experienced. Compassion. Tenderness. Hope. Is it random alignment? She thinks not. Someone orchestrated this all for her. How well thought out and lovingly intimate.

Refilling the jug of Half 'n Half, Dominic glances at the slight, brunette woman sitting by the window. He hasn't seen her before, and it being a small town, he notices. As he watches her looking at her coffee cup and the yellow lollipop she chose, he sees her eyes are over-bright and misted. There is deep emotion at play here, and he feels like an intruder watching her.

As Meredith brushes past her on the way to the stock room, Dominic hears the woman tell Meredith how beautiful the foam balloon looks and how much she appreciates her decorating her coffee with something so precious. Hmm. Interesting way to describe a foam design…

Dominic hears the woman push back her chair and gather her purse, coffee, and lollipop. She stands a moment, then shyly approaches him.

"Hi, excuse me—where did you find these lollipops? I know this sounds silly, but they bring back some good memories for me, and I really needed that today. So, anyway, thanks."

She hurries from the café and out onto the street. Dominic stands still for a few minutes taking in what she said. So, this is what the feelings of anticipation and purpose were about this morning; the reason these silly, spunky lollipops caught his eye, willing him to display them. Someone arranged this random encounter for a dark-haired woman who needed a reminder of good things and happy times. Standing in the middle of The Cuppa Café, Dominic smiles to himself. Who knew that latte foam and lollipops could be life-changing?

# …in Nature

# My Garden

MY GARDEN is a quiet place, my tranquil oasis that beckons when mind and body are overwhelmed, parched, and in need of peace. The haphazard, random way I choose the spot for each plant may appear chaotic to the more organized and regimented soul. For me, I find immense peace and joy in the random and untamed order of it all. There is peace and rest in the chaos.

The purple Catmint and Lantana, along with the bright yellow Yarrow, are a riot of tumbling blooms that spread as they wish, seeming to luxuriate in their boldness to overtake what they will. The white Guara, reaching high, looks like little butterflies dancing about on the wavy stems. The gentle Lavender is unassuming and lovely yet dominates its corner of the garden. The Sage, Fuchsia, Freesia, Primrose, and Geranium show off gorgeous splashes of purples, reds, pinks, and yellows, while the stately Ferns are calming with their greenery. A favorite scent of Jasmine wafts in the air as it climbs the fence and trellis.

There are fairies, angels, memorials to beloved pets, and random garden décor that also grace my garden. Seeing them peeking out from around a mass of flowers makes me smile. The unexpected amid chaos and beauty…

Chattering and bubbly, the three-tier fountain splashes and soothes. The water cascades down the pineapple-shaped top tier, beckoning birds to take a sip and a bath. It's calming to watch and listen as they bathe, call, and survey the garden, hunting for choice grubs and seeds. Two more birdbaths are placed throughout the yard to host birds, as well as squirrels, opossums, bees, and neighborhood cats.

The tall, purple-bloomed Butterfly Bush and the Fuji apple tree provide shade for the stone bench underneath their branches. It's in another part of the garden which provides a different perspective; one can feel hidden while resting there.

When it's time to prune, the honeybees and large black and yellow bumblebees allow me access to their plants while keeping a sharp eye on my activity. Some fly up near my head and hover there, inspecting me and gauging my intentions. Respect and harmony in the garden.

Sitting at the wooden picnic table, I watch the garden life and activity. Nourishment, community, rest, and safety happen here as God's creatures bathe, pollinate, eat, and gossip—doing what they were made to do. I love being part of it in my little slice of nature.

Perhaps if you close your eyes, you will hear the chatter of the birds as they gossip, sip, and search for breakfast along the fence and under the flowers. Maybe you will discover a hidden fairy or turtle and see the busy bees flitting with purpose from bloom to bloom. The perky splash of the fountain might soothe and restore peace to your soul. Some of the heaviness you carry might lift as you listen to the bold, russet squirrels scolding the big, black crows over peanuts with the scent of Jasmine swirling around you in the puffy breeze.

The tinkling wind chimes add their flavor of peace as all the elements of the garden blend beautifully, order yet chaos, to bring serenity and restoration to a tired soul. The Creator uses this small oasis in the middle of a neighborhood to blend the right mix of joy, rest, peace and chuckles at creature antics to refresh and restore the spirit. Now it's time to begin the day and hide in my heart the peace and refreshment I found in my garden.

# Something About the Rain

THERE'S SOMETHING lovely about the rain. The moment those first drops touch your face, hair, and eyes. Refreshing. Joyful.

Hearing the gentle thrum on the patio cover in the wee morning hours, pattering and plopping, is like a sky song flowing down. So soothing. Blankets envelop me in warmth and safety as I drowse and listen to nature's lullaby.

The muted sky and rain-damp air offer the unmistakable scent of cleanness as the Earth is washed, rinsed, and rejuvenated. It is a gentle yet fierce and unrelenting opening of the heavens—the Creator gifting a new start and a clean slate. Life-giving water. Living water.

The faithful pattering, dripping, and beating of good steady rain soothes the spirit and often my hectic mind with nature's rhythms—an intentional chorus on repeat. The weight of cares and worries lift as the rain sluices off the debris and detritus of humanity.

Something about the rain dredges up childhood memories of wildly exciting, terrifying thunder and lightning storms with windows rattling and trembling. Such an electric feeling of exhilaration, fear, and joy, intertwining emotions that shouldn't mix well together, but they do. Untamed and elemental.

Childhood memories drift up of hot summer days when a sudden rainstorm cooled and refreshed with the unforgettable scent of rain on hot sidewalks—drippy, melting popsicles created a sticky rainbow of colors along our faces and arms, held out to the rain to wash and streak our skin.

Something about rain and the wind that dashes trees and scatters leaves is a reminder that not everything in life is predictable and controllable. It's not tamable, quieted, or soothed but roars, bucks, and thrashes at the whim of the One who commands it. The beauty and raw power are thrilling, terrifying, and beautiful as nature follows the Creator's bidding—a God gift that I treasure. The mystery of it speaks to my soul. There is just something about the rain…

# Meadow

STANDING at the edge of the alpine meadow, my coffee mug is warm in my hands. A beautiful balance to the chill air. Ahhh…

Under the towering Sugar Pines, I take a few moments to soak in the first glimpse. My senses are awake and receptive, drinking it in. There is a physical sensation of being pulled and beckoned, compelling me to go out in the meadow. This is my place. Belonging.

Leisurely walking the boardwalk, I notice the sights, sounds, and smells that make up this lovely place. Earthy, elemental, fresh, yet ancient is what comes to mind. I pause and deeply breathe in the air cleansed by so many Sugar Pines, Giant Sequoias, and Cedars.

The meadow is already alive with creatures going about their business. The shiny black birds and bright, bold Tanagers call, dive, and swoop as they greet each other and share the meadow gossip. Flitting insects and seeds make up their breakfast. They light on the tip top of the purple-blue lupine, singing and swaying with the breeze ruffling the meadow flowers and leafy plants. Joyful!

There is a greyed and hollowed-out fallen tree with gnarled branches and bits of decayed roots lying across part of the meadow. A small tree is growing up from the edge of one of the dead branches. I wonder what creatures call the nooks and crannies home. Grasses in varying shades of green, bright yellow Sneezeweed, tiny white flowers, and deep purple lupines have grown up around the old tree like an embrace. These colorful flowers create a gorgeous living carpet. Breathtaking.

Walking further in, I find the perfect spot to sit. Settling in, I am at peace. A feeling of being welcomed, rooted, and folded in as if I belong here, in sync with the mystery and rhythm of the meadow. Connected.

I hear a rustling scurry in the clump of meadow flowers just below and to the left of my spot. A small grey-brown head peeks up and watches me, judging and spying. Deeming me safe, the chipmunk darts across the boardwalk, continuing his morning journey. I'm curious about what the day holds for it. Purpose.

Trickling and whispering, a little stream bubbles and flows out into the meadow. Tiny insects dip and float on the clear water. Other creatures scratch and rustle in the crowded marshy earth, searching for an appetizing addition to their breakfast. I don't know its source, but as the season pushes on, the stream will slow, and the water will pool, creating a new habitat that sustains those late summer and early fall plants, flowers, and creatures. Seasons.

The morning light filters through the tree branches at the edge of the meadow, casting a mysterious, divine glow as the summer sun rises. The rays force their way between thick, pinecone-laden branches burnishing the meadow with a lemony, pure, white light. Each light ray is distinct and discernable, stretching out beyond the trees to touch a specific spot. These bold rays are in sharp contrast to the meadow area still in shadows. The lighting produces an ethereal, otherworldly feeling where one might fancy seeing a forest sprite or fairy dancing and flitting through old growth and flowers. A supernatural spotlight.

The Divine is palpable and alive in this place. The Creator is here in this beautiful meadow. It is ancient ways, knowledge, and mystery, the connection between living things and continuous rebirth.

The cool morning air is becoming warmer as the sun continues its climb. I have been out here for a while, feeling as one with nature and this meadow. The early morning creature energy is slowing to a lazier, relaxed pace, slipping into the routine and warmth of the late morning and early afternoon.

It is time to get on with the day. I feel melancholy and wistful as my time in the meadow comes to an end for this trip. Life will go on uninterrupted after I head down the mountain. It is as if I'm leaving part of myself here with the meadow to be picked up on my next visit to recharge and restore what life has depleted. Is it strange to feel so connected to a place?

Divine connections and encounters are a blessing. It feels like hope. I will treasure these sights, scents, and sounds until next time when I sense the meadow's welcoming arms and soothing call to come and sit for a while.

# Whirlwind

THERE IS a restless, unsettled energy hovering around my heart and soul this morning as I take that first anticipated sip of coffee. The dark, earthy scent is familiar and safe, an old and expected routine. Yet, the familiarity is not calming and soothing this morning, and that throws me off-kilter.

Watching the critter activity from my kitchen window, the steaming coffee warming my hands, I am reminded of the power nature possesses to soothe, hush, and calm my spirit. It's where I talk to You and hear You speak to me. Healing. Peace.

Time to get outside!

Donning a hoodie with Pacific Northwest on the front, I grab a hat. I choose the one that says *Sorta Sweet, Sorta Savage*. That's how I feel this morning. Restless, savage, a bit wild in the heart. I need movement.

The park with the pond is beautiful this morning. The geese are already up, fussing and snipping at the grass, finding their favorite delicacies. Their contented honks and bossy hissing are pleasant and funny. The routine of it calms and soothes. My chilled hands unclench just a bit.

A big white egret is sunning itself as it hunts. It stands on its thin, nimble legs on a jumble of rocks in a corner of the pond, motionless yet always watching for the slightest movement of its next meal. The egret shares this rock with another pond dweller catching some morning sun. Always vigilant and suspicious, the large pond turtle appears to be oblivious to me, but I know it isn't. I'm being carefully monitored.

Brilliant blue sky above me, dew-damp grass under my feet, and a spunky breeze skipping around the pond—the perfect morning.

On the other side of the pond, the trees are showing off their gorgeous autumn colors. The vivid oranges and reds blend and blur with the yellows and greens like a startling tableau of beauty and peace. I take a few moments at the edge of the pond to soak it in. The sight is majestic, bold, and insistent—the contrasting loveliness of the bright blue sky and these gorgeous colors demand all my focus and attention. There is strength and defiance in the colors and tenacious hold these trees have on their foliage as they shout their last hurrah before letting go and descending into rest, quiet, and rebirth at the change of season. It must happen. The change is inevitable, predicted, and set into motion by Your design. Letting go is part of life as it unrelentingly moves forward. I see that as I take in the trees and seasonal changes at the pond. It brings some comfort to my troubled and agitated heart.

This is a season of many changes, and I'm forced to find

my way into a new normal. I don't like it, and it frightens me. I struggle and kick, even though I know it will happen despite my stubborn clinging. I feel a bit savage about letting go. Unsettled. Unknown. Defiant.

Moving along the edge of the pond, I look up through the stunning leaf color and pause to breathe deeply. I sense You here with me. Cleansing. Surrender. Beauty. Safe.

You are here in the season of rebirth and new life and the season of release and rest. It is incessant, this change of season. It is needed, necessary, and it will happen. My shoulders slowly drop, and my back relaxes as You speak to my soul and minister to my heart. You remind me there is beauty in letting go. It is the precursor to a season of change, growth, and intimacy with You. The status quo never brings the exciting feeling of a new chapter and fresh adventures. You have more in store for me. My purpose on Earth is continually moving—being blown by Your breath and Your plan. The journey to get there involves upheaval and letting go. Trust. Intimacy. Faith.

The spunky breeze is back and becoming a bit more playful in its bluster. Resuming my walk, I am suddenly caught up in a whirlwind of brightly finished leaves and brown grasses, whirling and tossing and pulling at my hat. Laughing, I raise my arms and let it dart, tease and play! Zipping and dancing all around me and sticking to my sleeves, the leaves embrace the wildness and seemingly random whim of the wind and let go.

It is magical, beautiful, and joyful! My heart responds and softens, restlessness and fear melting away. "Can I trust You with me, Lord?" I ask in the wind.

"Absolutely!" the leaves reply as they dash away in freedom on the adventure You created for them.

# Memories

ALL IS QUIET for the moment in the forest and meadow surrounding the cabin. A gentle breath of wind shushes through the meadow grasses and whispers through the pine branches.

Pink and orangey-yellow streaks are breaking just above the treetops announcing that the sun is on its way. Nature's alarm clock. Soon the morning creatures will stir, scout, and begin their breakfast journeys.

Warming pine and that distinctive mountain scent waft and swirl, and I am reminded of long-ago summer mornings at a favorite campground in the mountains. I can see, hear, and smell it all in my mind—the bossy scrub jays shouting and squawking as they flit from tree to tree cocking an alert black eye at the wooden campground table in case some of the breakfast fixings tumble off. The smokey scent of the testy, cold campfire that fights to get going again in the morning reminds me of my dad, who would mess with it until it was hot and roaring, so we could toast some crescent rolls on a stick over the fire.

Steamy coffee warms my chilled hands as I sit on the deck overlooking the drowsy meadow. The sun is higher now, and beautiful streaks of sunlight boldly push through the tree branches. The rays of light are ethereal and sacred, the Creator at work bringing beauty to the morning. The way the magical light beams fall on the meadow and through the trees reminds me of times spent hiking—just He and I—where hurts and wounds were poured out in raw honesty and need as Truth and Healing flooded in to soothe, heal, and mend what was broken. Divine appointments..

Breakfast accompanies me to the deck. The homey scent of pancakes, bacon, and coffee, mingling with the scent of pine, sparks a memory of my grandma making breakfast on a Saturday morning. The scent of pine was always present and is a treasured undercurrent to many of my memories of her. How happy and exciting it felt to be in her home, surrounded by woods, good food, and squirrels' feet pattering across the roof. Safe. Home. Content.

The sun is making its way across the sky. It's time for a hike to the lake to see who is stirring and fussing about this morning. Always an adventure!

The strewn pine needles are soft and comfy underfoot. Cracks, snaps, and rustling along the edges and further into the forest accompany me as I make my way along the well-worn path. The rustlings, chirps, and murmurs of the woods and its inhabitants are comforting and peaceful. Nature is quiet, but it's not. Calm and restful, yet busy and purposeful as the birds and watchful animals go about their business.

There it is—the lake! Life is in full swing, with ducks and geese gliding along the smooth, still water, snipping at bugs, and nibbling grasses along the shore. Their contented chuckles, and murmurs drift over the water as they chat over their breakfast.

A creature rambling through the reeds makes slippery, muddy sounds along the bank of the lake near an ancient tree. A long-abandoned rope swing, frayed, tattered, and limp, tosses meekly in the light breeze that's beginning to ruffle the water.

Sitting under the shady branches with the fishy, watery scent of the lake breeze fluffing my hair, I recall the excitement of fishing along the banks of another lake in the mountains with my grandpa. The careful choosing of the bait, adding weights, and a bright red bobber. Time seemed to slow as the line was cast, reeled, and repeated over the course of a warm summer afternoon. The same breeze with an earthy, fishy lake water scent kept the worst of the heat at bay.

Feeling dozy, I lie on the blanket I brought and close my eyes for a while. The earthy smell of the lake combined with the close warmth of the afternoon fills my mind with peace, and I nap for a bit; childhood memories of cloud-watching and camping take me away.

Startled by the fussy chatter of a grey squirrel in the branches above, I stretch and gather up my things to head back. What a beautiful way to spend a lazy afternoon. Looking at the sky, I see the sun is beginning to make its descent.

Relaxing on the deck after a quick dinner of grilled chicken and homemade potato salad, I sip a lovely cup of herbal tea as the sun showcases its final burst of color before setting behind the treetops.

The forest and meadow quiet into the evening as the first pinprick stars make their appearance. As the night gentles and cools, I grab the old quilt off the chair. It feels safe to be wrapped up and warm. There are unknowns and mysteries and strange sounds moving around me in the dark forest, but I don't feel afraid. Gazing up at the stars, a feeling of being deeply loved washes over me. You created these stars and heavenly bodies, placing them just so in the night sky, giving direction to the weary traveler, bringing light to the one who feels lost. When I felt tiny and insignificant in a vast sea of humanity, You reached out to me with lovely bursts of light breaking through the darkness. You spoke to my soul of hope, purpose, and safety. You still see me. The lovely carpet of stars in the night sky continues to speak of love, peace, and warmth on the quiet deck of a cabin in the woods. Beautiful memories of healing and redemption and, above all, hope.

# ...in Ordinary Life

# Nostalgia

IT'S GOING to be a hot day, so I'm up early. I head to the patio with my warm coffee. There is a slight chill, oh so slight, that I feel on my skin.

There is something vague and wistful in the way the air feels this morning. A hint of warmth to come, mixed with that slight chill. It feels so familiar.

It's the way the light is coming up over the apple tree, shadows from the branches falling just so on the green grass touching the edges of the three-tiered fountain. The yellowy-white light pulls at my memory; I've seen this light before. I know it.

I hear it in the way the finches, bold blue jays, and grey tit-mouse call and chatter. Fuzzy squirrels scampering and digging in the grass and garden tug at something hovering in my mind.

The scent in the air has a subtle, comforting, reminiscent quality to it that dances on the fringe of my memory. It is happy and calming, stirring up a sentimental longing and wistful affection for something…is it a specific memory or snippets of various memories stirred up by the sight, sound, or scent of this peaceful morning? I wonder…

Sitting at the pine table, I allow my thoughts the freedom to go where they will.

The scents, light, and creature sounds call up memories of my grandparents' house in Lakehead, CA. I loved this place! It was nestled in and around pine trees with squirrels and birds galore! I recall the warm, safe scent of those pine trees, the dusty earth, and the bubbling excitement of walking through the wooded area to the little market with my grandma. Adventure!

In the warm afternoons, the blue kiddie pool was set up in the backyard under some shady pine trees. Buckets, cups, Barbies, and various other toys made for a fun and easy afternoon. I think time stood still for a bit. My grandma sat in the shade on her 70's era lawn chair with a sweating glass of sweet tea and chatted with me. Always the old, lovely scent of warm pine and earth. Safe.

I remember the thrill and exhilaration of hurtling down the big hill near their home in my little red wagon—the pine-y wind in my face. Freedom!

I enjoyed the lovely summer-night strolls to visit neighbors and see a few deer as we walked along, making our rounds. Pleasant and friendly.

Scampering squirrels on my fence remind me of the patter of squirrel feet running over the roof of their home and my grandpa's garage in the early mornings. The garage was a wonderful place. It was filled with gadgets, boxes of nails and rakes, fishing gear, and all sorts of fun things to play with and explore. It had the distinct smell of cars and the tangy scent of oil and gasoline. Order and routine, everything in its place.

I can still smell the fishy, earthy, watery scent of Lake Shasta where my grandpa, my dad, and I spent many hours on his boat fishing and motoring around the lake, stopping in the small, quiet coves to cool off and swim. Even in the summer heat, there was the distinct lake chill that danced above the water. Dinner of freshly caught fish gave me a warm, homey feeling. We ate dinner on the enclosed porch at the picnic table, talking and laughing about the highlights of the day. As the adults talked on into the summer night, I would drowse and daydream.

Yes, these are cherished memories. Interesting how a subtle scent in the air, a ray of sunlight, and nature sounds have the power to trigger the mind and bring these memories flooding back.

I wish I could go back and relive those parts of life, recapturing the feelings and sensations. Happy memories of pleasant times when life seemed simpler, sweeter, and less complex. I often experience this around the holidays when looking at old pictures of family gathered around a festive table, carving a pumpkin, or sitting by the Christmas tree. When I look at paintings of the holidays in times past, there is a wistful, yearning feeling of wanting to be there. Nostalgia.

Life is chaotic and unpredictable. I wonder if our adult brains unconsciously seek out the sights, scents, and sounds of a time when things were ordered, reliable, safe, and predictable. I believe God wired us to treasure and preserve those moments. We can pull them from our heart memories as comfort and a break from the monotony and loneliness of life.

I pray that nostalgia visits me often, like an old, dear friend, full of comfort, comradery, and memories to make me smile. What a gift!

# Roads and Rivers

Isaiah 43:19 "Forget about what's happened; don't keep going over old history. Be alert, be present. I'm about to do something brand-new. It's bursting out! Don't you see it? There it is! I'm making a road through the desert, rivers in the badlands."

I tend to revisit the past and analyze it to death. I become consumed with situations, words spoken that hurt (either by me or to me), and actions that I fear will happen again and again. Isaiah's words say to forget about reliving all that and be alert and present. I do not want to miss the brand-new things God is planning to do. He isn't saying, "I'd like to do something new" or "I'm considering it." No!

He says, "I am about to do something brand-new!" It is a promise! I can feel His excitement breaking through when He says, "Don't you see it? There it is!" The Lord is wild about us and loves the plans He has so masterfully created for us. I imagine it brings Him such pleasure to surprise us with His purpose for our lives and to whisper into our spirits, "This is the way; walk in it."

If I stay tangled up in the past or worry over the future, I will miss what He is doing right this minute. I want to fully experience the road He is making through my desert, the obstacles He will move, and the ruts He will smooth over. Imagine looking back and seeing how it all unfolded! Some days it feels like I can't find the road because there are too many offshoots and rabbit holes that distract and keep me spinning. If I stop, breathe, and give myself space and permission to spend time with Him, He reveals the path and gives wisdom about how to get back to it. He helps me over the ruts, around the boulders, and through the brambles. He reveals the beauty that is there.

How bleak to miss the rushing river of blessings and revelation that He is creating in the badlands I often roam! How quickly I forget that water is the source of life. Where there is water, there is beauty, refreshment, life, and provision. Jesus is my river in the badlands of humanity. He is beautiful, my strength, my peace; He refreshes my soul and provides everything I need. He is the source of life, and He is enough. How wise I would be if I lived with this mindset every day. So, let's be alert! Let's watch and wait to see what He will do in our deserts and badlands. There is joy and beauty He wants to show us on our journey. May we live in watchful expectation.

# Jesus with Skin On

ARE YOU familiar with the expression "Jesus with skin on?" I once heard the analogy explained in this way which made a lot of sense.

When Jesus, who was fully man and fully God, was born into this world, He literally had skin on, human flesh, and blood. He intimately knows what it means to be us. He understands hunger, pain, grief, sunshine on His face, exhaustion, fellowship with others, belly laughs, and joy. Since we are created in His image, we can learn to act like Him as we interact with our fellow sojourners on this journey of life.

So, what might that look like? We see Jesus spending time with people who did not have it all together. They lied, cheated, and were selfish; they were ill and in physical and emotional pain. He surrounded Himself with those who had mouths like sailors, drank too much, and did things they regretted. These are the people with whom Jesus spent a lot of time. People just like us.

What did He do? He spoke to them. He healed them, fed

them, and listened to them. Jesus spoke truth in love. Jesus didn't shy away from them when they were rejected and shunned from society. He didn't tolerate sin and pretend it didn't exist. He called it out and forgave it. He saw them and their potential, and He LOVED THEM.

How might it look for us to be Jesus with skin on? Smile and acknowledge the existence of someone struggling, who might not be as clean as you prefer and might use words that offend you. Jesus loves them. Have respect and compassion for those you encounter who act and dress in ways you don't like. Bring meals to those who are dealing with a job loss, illness, or death in the family. Give someone your warm jacket or umbrella when they are stuck in the rain. Listen to the one who's hurting. Seek them out. It is ok to be with people who may not believe the way you do or who don't believe in anything at all. He deeply loves them.

I have learned a lot about being Jesus with skin on from my two children, now adults. One afternoon they came from a little shopping center near our home with stories of the homeless woman they talked to, who poured out her sadness over the loss of her husband. They were young teens at the time and didn't know exactly what to do, so they bought her lunch, listened to her, and told her they hoped she would be ok. The woman cried because no one else cared or even saw her. Jesus with skin on—kindness.

There was the time my daughter rushed home from 7/11, grabbed a backpack, and filled it with non-perishables from the pantry, water bottles, a gift card, blankets, and other items she found in her room and gave it to a man she met who needed help. Jesus with skin on—compassion.

Or my son, who regularly gives money, help, or food to those he crosses paths with that could use a hand. That is Jesus with skin on—generosity.

It isn't hard, but it does require us to look beyond outward appearances and find the one that Jesus loves so deeply. He gave up His life for them, just like He did for you. My hope is that we all will find someone in our spheres to love—to show them Jesus.

# Beauty

PSALM 139:13-18 "You made all the delicate, inner parts of my body and knit me together in my mother's womb. Thank you for making me so wonderfully complex! Your workmanship is marvelous—how well I know it. You watched me as I was being formed in utter seclusion, as I was woven together in the dark of the womb. You saw me before I was born. Every day of my life was recorded in your book. Every moment was laid out before a single day had passed. How precious are your thoughts about me, O God. They cannot be numbered! I can't even count them; they outnumber the grains of sand! And when I wake up, you are still with me."

So much is hurled at us about our outward appearance; our size, eye and hair color, skin tone, you name it—society has decided what is acceptable, and it is terribly flawed and destructive.

Think for a moment about something that is unique to you. Is it your laugh, smile, eye, or hair color? Do you have a unique sense of style or a quirky sense of humor? This unique part of you is a gift from God that was carefully thought out. It sets you apart as special. Imagine the conversations that took place in Heaven about you; the smile on the Creator's face as He looked at His finished and perfected workmanship, you, and deemed you a beautiful masterpiece declaring you are created in His image. Will you look at your uniqueness and love it? Ephesians 2:10 says, "For we are all God's masterpiece. He created us anew in Christ Jesus so that we can do the good things He planned for us long ago."

Just as the Creator carefully planned each of your physical traits, He gifted you with inner beauty and the characteristics of Jesus—kindness, inclusivity, compassion, mercy, humility, and forgiveness. These traits have the power to draw people to you because they see Jesus shining through the vessel of your physical body. We have a God-sized space in our souls that longs to be known, loved, and accepted. Only God can fill that void. The more we look like Jesus on the inside, the more beautiful we become on the outside.

Think about the traits of inner beauty that you have been gifted with. Are you patient and laid back, or are you a confident, type-A go-getter? Perhaps you are kind and merciful. A dreamer or a realist? Maybe you are humble and gentle. Do you have compassion for those less fortunate? All these qualities are gifts given to you by a loving God who knows your strengths and weaknesses.

If you struggle to see yourself as a beautiful creation, a one-of--a-kind work of art, ask God to be your mirror. Ask Him to reflect back to you the beauty and loveliness He sees when He looks at you. He sees all the potential He placed in you. There is only one you, and you are enough.

Zephaniah 3:17 "The Lord your God is with you; His power gives you victory. The Lord will take delight in you, and in His love, He will give you new life. He will sing and be joyful over you."

# People Watching

Sitting downtown at the park with my Peets cappuccino, I settle in to observe people, one of my favorite pastimes. There is so much to learn through the countless ways people express themselves and interact with others.

There are several paved paths in the park, allowing walkers and runners to take different routes each time they go around the square. It is interesting to see the path each person chooses. Some strictly follow the square path circling the park and do not deviate from that. Others choose a different intersecting path each time, making their jaunt around the park unpredictable to those observing them. Different personalities at play.

From my bench, I spot a group of 60-something ladies in their comfy walking outfits, white shoes, and brightly colored sun visors. They walk two to three abreast, loudly chatting about the choices their grown children and grandchildren are making. The ladies appear oblivious to the rest of the parkgoers as they march in serious conversation peppered with laughter stemming from a long-time camaraderie.

These ladies must know each other and the inner workings of each family on a deep level to have earned the right to share their opinions. It's entertaining to guess how they first met and the careful dance they did around each other until familiarity, trust, and love grew into the friendship they now share. I want friendships like this—women who have a place in my heart that is so woven and interconnected that we weather all kinds of storms and victories together, never hesitating to rally around each other with love, laughter, encouragement, and respect. I am grateful for the precious women that fill this spot. I say a prayer for those I'm blessed to call friends.

Across the square, four or five teens are hanging out at one of the tables. Backpacks, phones, and food are strewn between them as they take selfies, gossip, and laugh at TikTok videos. One young lady appears to lead the pack. When she laughs, the others laugh, and when she stands up to dance to a favorite song, all eyes are on her, and a couple of them get up and mimic her dancing. She is the first to grab the snacks, and the others defer. Interesting how different personality types drift together; the leaders and followers, the outgoing and introverts, all have a place. As I observe them, I wonder what God's plan is for them. They each have unique gifts and talents. It is easy to watch a strong type-A leader and imagine them going far, but sometimes it's the quiet observers who take the world by storm. I pray that they each find their place and people; that there is always someone in their corner who supports and loves them deeply.

Next to the water fountain, an older man takes a break from his walk. He follows the same paved path for each turn around the park. This is not the first time I have seen him here walking his predictable route. He walks with purpose but at a slow pace. His comfortable shoes and tan slacks with a t-shirt are his usual outfit. As he sits a spell, I notice him looking at each person as they move past him, as if willing them to notice him and spend a few minutes shooting the breeze. I'm close enough to see his wistful gaze—maybe he remembers other walks in this park, perhaps with his wife or a close friend that he has since lost. Are nostalgia and memories his close friends now? It gives me an ache in my heart for him. I imagine Jesus next to him on the dark blue bench bringing him comfort, peace, and a balm for his loneliness. The ultimate best friend. I say a prayer for this gentleman, asking for some joy, peace, and camaraderie.

As the morning moves along, the playground fills with moms and kids. Different parenting styles are evident this morning, and I find it fascinating. There is the group on one side of the playground, who have taken up an entire section of the granite bench that encircles the play area. They are so orderly and neat! Snacks, tiny water bottles, and juice-filled cups are lined up carefully. Each child is told to get a big drink and stay hydrated before going on their climbing, shrieking, energy-draining adventures. Most obey and have big drinks, except for a couple of them, who cannot resist the pull of play. They peek at their moms, take the tiniest, fastest sip possible and dash off. These moms seem to enjoy their time together, but always with a sharp eye on all the shenanigans happening on the slide and big climbing tunnels.

I hear warnings of, "Be careful, slow down, that's too high, and use your words!" shouted from the bench, all the while still managing to maintain the flow of conversation.

Another pair of moms and kids occupy a spot next to the well-organized group. These moms have a couple of backpacks full of random snacks, toys, and juice boxes spilling out. They are more carefree in their playground rules. I hear fewer shouts and warnings from these two. They are intent on their conversation, less focused on the playground interactions, and the children are quick to take advantage.

The children and their interactions with each other are so interesting. I love how the lone child there with his mom is included in the games and treated as if he has been part of their group forever. Easy inclusion; no posturing and judging. Adults could learn a lot from that.

Looking at these little lives, I imagine the mark each of these children will leave on the world. I ask God to smooth out and make their paths straight, to open doors that keep them going in the right direction, and for His hand of protection to be all over them.

Under the leafy trees next to the pathway lies a homeless man wrapped in his sleeping bag. He isn't sleeping. His arms are behind his head, and he looks up into the leafy foliage. A suitcase full of his belongings and life is settled next to him, along with a water bottle and a crumpled chip bag. I watch as the park walkers notice him there. The reactions are varied. A woman with her coffee and small bag of something yummy from Peets changes direction and follows a different route. Is it to avoid passing him? Does she fear having to acknowledge him or worry she will be asked for something? Others pass him by without a second glance, intent on the path in front of them or their phones. I can tell they are very aware of him but don't want it to be known. Are they afraid of what they don't understand and haven't experienced? Is it fear? What if the person suffers from mental illness and acts erratically? What do they do then? How lonely and hurtful it is to be unseen.

Eventually, an older man and his dog stop and engage him. The dog sniffs and wags as the man pets and interacts, maybe for the first time in a while. After their pleasantries and chat are finished, I watch the man's face. He looks after the one who stopped and made him feel seen. His face reflects that joy of acknowledgment, and it's a lovely thing to see. Who knows what that simple act will do for this man and his life trajectory? We never know for certain what our interaction with another human being does for them, but we can rest assured there is an effect, either positive or negative, never neutral. I offer a prayer for provision, protection, and opportunity for his circumstances to change.

There are frequently lone walkers in this park. They seem to be tranquil and at peace on the outside, but I wonder what burdens lie on their hearts. A few take a seat on benches and watch the world go by. Maybe they are taking advantage of a few moments alone to recharge. Maybe they are on a break, getting in some steps, or waiting to meet a friend.

As I sit, I wonder if there are fellow people watchers quietly observing me. Are they trying to divine what I'm about, what my facial expressions and body language are speaking, and what my heart holds? I wonder if they can tell that I'm a fellow observer trying to glean insight into the human spirit.

Psalm 139:2-3 says, "You know when I sit down and when I rise up; you discern my thoughts from afar. You search out my path, and my lying down and are acquainted with all my ways."

God is the ultimate people watcher. He sees, knows, and discerns everything we are about and all that hurts us and heals us. It makes me happy to know how carefully watched over and known I am. We only see what people choose to reveal and try to discern what it all means, but God…He knows our inner workings and sees past the persona we offer to the world and the parts we so desperately want to hide. To be fully known and greatly adored is relief, rest, and peace.

# What do you Want?

"WHAT DO YOU WANT?" is a generic question most of us hear at least once a day. Maybe we are the ones asking it when plans, relationships, and circumstances do not line up with our hopes and expectations or when something blindsiding pops up, and we don't know how to react.

As this question simmers and swirls in my brain, I realize what I long for most I already have in Jesus. I already have it. Read those words again. This goes further than the physical want of food, water, and clothing. This question pleads with us to go deeper. You know the place where putting words to the emotion, need, and longing is almost impossible, yet it is there and desperate to be heard. God uses this un-nameable want to draw us to Him because it keeps us seeking Him. We may not have the words, but our souls know Him and long for everything He provides.

What do you long for most and think you don't have? Security and safety? A friend? Do you feel anonymous in a big, wide world? Maybe you want to know you are fully known and loved unconditionally. Perhaps you crave order and chaos in a world that is wildly out of order.

You have all these things! You are safe and secure, though at times, it can be hard to believe. Things do not always work out the way we plan, dream, and hope. Jobs are still lost, loved ones still pass, friendships still end, children still make choices that break our hearts, and disease still knocks on our doors.

This is where faith, trust, and hope live, in the parts of life that do not make sense, that are chaotic, frightening, and painful. This is where the tiniest shards of belief must reside; the belief that nothing touches you without first being filtered through His scarred hands—hands that were scarred to seal you to Him and to make eternal life with Him possible. He does see you. He hears you and knows your every thought.

Zephaniah 3:17 tells you that "The Lord your God is in your midst; a mighty one who will save; he will rejoice over you with gladness; he will quiet you by his love; he will exult over you with loud singing."

The Creator took such time, tender care, and attention as you were created and the breath of life breathed into your lungs. His breath in your lungs. You have a purpose. Jeremiah 29:11 says, "For I know the plans I have for you," declares the Lord, "plans to prosper you and not to harm you, plans to give you hope and a future." Jesus desires to bring order, calm, and peace into every circumstance. In the toughest situations life throws at you, He is right there offering you His love, offering you Himself. His wisdom is available, as is His peace if you ask Him.

Think deeply about what it is you think you don't have, what you long for the most, and ask Him to show you that you have it. Be ready! It may show up in unexpected, surprising places that delight you, bringing joy and rest from all the striving and searching you have been doing for so long.

# Sowing and Reaping

GALATIANS 6:7-10 "Don't be misled: No one makes a fool of God. What a person plants, he will harvest. The person who plants selfishness, ignoring the needs of others—ignoring God!—harvests a crop of weeds. All he'll have to show for his life is weeds! But the one who plants in response to God, letting God's Spirit do the growth work in him, harvests a crop of real life, eternal life. So, let's not allow ourselves to get fatigued doing good. At the right time, we will harvest a good crop if we don't give up or quit. Right now, therefore, every time we get the chance, let us work for the benefit of all, starting with the people closest to us in the community of faith."

While sipping my coffee this morning, I came across the above verse in Galatians. "What a person plants, he will harvest." Hmm. The words "will harvest" do not give any wiggle room, do they? The Apostle Paul was not mincing words when he penned this verse. We WILL harvest what we plant. If we choose to plant acid words, toxic behavior, and selfishness, we WILL harvest these very things in our lives. The very things we desperately want to avoid. What are we planting, and do we like what that harvest will produce and reproduce?

Imagine with me a typical day. Each of us has myriad opportunities to plant good things, but will we?

We wake up tired and irritated due to a sleepless night. We throw ourselves out of bed, mentally ticking off all the things we must do. Our tread is heavy and annoyed as we head to the kitchen for our coffee. Waiting for it to brew, we decide it is unfair that everyone else sleeps soundly in our house, and we become increasingly irritated noticing dirty dishes in the sink. The injustice of it all makes us choose to be noisier than necessary as we prepare coffee, feed the animals, and shove the offending dishes around in the sink. Making noise that might wake up the sound sleepers, which it does. This pervasive annoyance follows and taints the rest of the morning as we get ready for the day. We have already decided it is going to stink and be full of further difficulties and irritations. The seeds are planted, and we unknowingly begin our harvest. Our encounters with others will have a ripple effect with lasting repercussions.

Sitting at a stop light, we refuse to let another driver merge in front of us who found herself in the wrong lane; too bad for them, we think. Our rude stare and aggressive driving make us feel justified yet intensifies our frustration. Our actions plant seeds of fear, defensiveness, and worry in the woman to whom we refused to give a seed of grace. This hurtful exchange will travel with her as she goes about her day, spreading to everyone in her sphere. The ripple effect. It is powerful.

At the grocery store, our demeanor is aloof and unreachable. The older man in the aisle with us attempts a friendly chat about the soup he is going to make for his lunch and how he enjoys good bread with that soup. We refuse to engage and throw an insincere half-smile his way, mumble nonsense, and forcefully steer our cart further down the aisle, leaving him feeling wounded and humiliated. Who has time for idle blabbing when we are tired and annoyed? Ripples.

In the checkout line, we queue up behind a mom with two young kids. They are noisy and difficult. Arrogant and nasty, we loudly sigh, passive-aggressively showing offense and annoyance, exasperating an already frazzled Mama. She wonders if she is failing at mothering…more ripples. Sowing and reaping, the day goes on with anger, hopelessness, pain, and grief as our harvest. It is a vicious cycle and one we could have redeemed.

What might have happened had we chosen to plant different seeds? We might wake up tired and moody. We might not want to dig deep and change our perspective to view ourselves as gardeners to another's soul. That is tiring and hard and counter intuitive. But…we can vent all that frustration and exhaustion to our Father, who gives us strength and energy to plant seeds of hope, happiness, peace, and compassion.

The irritating driver in the wrong lane is on her way to a doctor's appointment, which has her terrified and unable to concentrate for fear of test results. Planting seeds of compassion and kindness by allowing her in front of us with a friendly wave and smile will vastly change the trajectory of her day. Our compassion might infuse her with peace, safety, and warm feelings of human kindness. A harvest of peace and compassion with lasting ripples.

The older man in the grocery store is suffering from deep grief and loneliness after the loss of his cherished wife. This was his first outing since her passing, and he simply needed to be seen, heard, and shown genuine kindness. By stopping to chat about how tasty soup and good bread can be, his loneliness is held at bay for a few minutes. Planting seeds of time, attention, kindness, and companionship grant him the confidence that he can do this; that he will be ok. He will know that he is seen, worth noticing, and not a forgotten, old face in a sea of humanity. A harvest of compassion, healing, and comfort that cost us a few moments.

The mom in the checkout line feels like a failure, like she cannot do this right and is not fit to be a mother. Planting seeds of compassion, encouragement, humor, and camaraderie in parenting let her know she is seen and understood, infusing her with confidence and patience with her children. Realizing she is doing a good job and is not alone and forgotten in this will completely rework the tone and outcome of the day for her and her children.

We get to choose how we interact with those God places in our path. We choose what seeds we plant. It is a choice, and it is not an easy one. It takes asking the One who is perfectly unselfish, perfectly compassionate, full of mercy, loving, and all-wise to give us His strength, discernment, and love.

I am grateful for the days that my family, friends, and total strangers make the choice to plant good things into my soul. The smile from a stranger, the friendly exchange over berries in the produce aisle, the text "Hey, thinking of you today," or an unexpected compliment on a day that is tough carry so much weight. Bad days are transformed in minutes by someone with a heart full of good seeds, who takes a moment to plant a few in mine. These seed planters will reap a harvest of goodness, generosity, compassion, and hope with the potential to reproduce one hundred-fold. This is the garden I want to be known for; one that produces good and makes a positive dent in my little sphere.

# …the Greatest Gift

# A Silent Night

THE CABIN is snug and cozy tonight.

Gently snoring, dogs on soft beds kick and yip as they dream of chasing the purring black cat nestled down and dozing on a warm blanket.

The fire glows brightly.

I watch the dancing colors mesmerize and hypnotize me from my favorite comfy chair; an old quilt jumbled around me. A steaming cup of tea warms the body and soul.

All is warm and pleasant.

The tree lights wink softly in the branches. It's magical and enchanting.

My wandering mind recalls vivid scenes of Christmases past—pine-scented memories of the perfect tree, glowing lights, and cherished ornaments sparkling as they peek out from their carefully chosen spot on the Christmas tree.

Fragrant mugs of creamy cocoa with floating marshmallows

mingle with the homey smells of holiday baking as Christmas carols sing out on the record player.

Memories of laughter and excited anticipation on Christmas Eve—Light of the world, blessed hope, holy and sacred.

The fire pops and crackles busily, snickering to itself as the peaceful evening flows on—past and present thoughts mix and blend, drowsy.

The distinctive sound of falling snow on this silent night.

# It Was Just a Night...

IMAGINE with me, if you will, what it may have been like for the shepherds on that holiest of nights, so many years ago.

The quiet hillside breathing silently under a clear, star-filled sky; the sound of their flocks settling in, like they always did, with murmurs, rustlings, and scrabbling with the occasional noisy bleat of lambs fussing for a warm spot next to the fluffy ewes.

Shepherds, ever watchful and alert, yet calm and ready for a typical, peaceful night. Perhaps they, too, scoot in close to the warm, fuzzy sheep as the night deepens and the air cools and chills.

Quiet conversations around a small fire and a simple meal, perhaps? Jokes and a recounting of the day wan and fade as the night falls deeper and silence blankets the hillside.

It was just a night until it wasn't...

Imagine their quiet night suddenly interrupted by the sky exploding in radiant, holy light and sound, like nothing ever seen before—certainly nothing ever seen by a group of tired shepherds outside a sleepy village on a typical night. The terror and fear must have been palpable, washing over them like a terrible nightmare, until they heard the angel's voice saying, "Don't be afraid! I bring you good news of great joy for everyone! The Savior—yes, the Messiah, the Lord—has been born tonight in Bethlehem, the City of David! And this is how you will recognize Him: You will find a baby lying in a manger, wrapped snugly in strips of cloth!"[1]

Add to this amazing announcement, this supernatural display, the addition of a vast host of the armies of heaven praising God and rejoicing at this beautiful, holy, saving gift just given to all people for all time. A gift that will never be fully understood—mocked, ridiculed, and murdered—yet the only gift that will love, redeem, and save your life and mine.

Imagine that first feeling of terror turning to incredible joy, unspeakable love, and supernatural peace that in all its Divine power was quite possibly unbearable—wild and fierce.

I can feel down to my very bones the uncontrollable need to fall to my knees in reverence, awe, fear, and worship before such an announcement! A Savior, the Messiah, the Holy One come to save—a divine encounter with the King of Kings and the heavenly host. The atmosphere must have been sizzling with a supernatural, divine portent.

When the angels departed, did the shepherds stand around arguing about what they experienced? Did they try to explain away this divine encounter with the supernatural as indigestion, an atmospheric distortion, strange cloud formations, or tainted wine? Did they minimize this gift of love so deep that human

---

1   Luke 2: 10-12

minds cannot fathom it? No, they didn't. They believed. They sought out the Savior to see Him, worship Him, and accept the love gift freely given to them. They accepted it and shared it with others.

I don't believe they slept much that night. Returning to their now still and silent hillside, I wonder if they spoke. Did they attempt to recount the events they had just witnessed? Did they fully understand the impact of what they beheld in that lowly stable? How does one explain the Divine? I wonder what changes took place silently in their hearts. Mary quietly treasured all she witnessed that night in her heart, and I believe the shepherds did the same.

It was just a night on a hillside with their sheep until it wasn't.

# December Moon

THE DECEMBER NIGHT is dark and deep, stillness and chill seeping into bones despite a layering of coat, scarf, hat, gloves, and thick-soled boots.

Footfall is muffled and shushed along the pine-strewn path, boots stirring up the ancient scent of the woods and winter--shrouded earth.

The hush of the forest has a particular sound—not truly silent to the careful observer but full of the rustle, scurry, and purpose of those living in the night. Frigid air gives their purpose a new vigor with warm dens and beds of fern, pine needles, and forest detritus waiting to give shelter.

Deep, full inhalations fill lungs to the brim with invigorating, life-giving air. Oddly, the heavy chill, though it burns and startles, offers peace and affirmation of knowing one is alive and well. Sometimes it takes the cloak of a dark, wintry, forest-y night to bring clarity to the chaos and exposure of living in the light.

Rounding the curve in the path, the stillness of the pond with the shimmery moon-glow trail on the dark water is breathtaking. A path of light and love painted on the water by the brush strokes of One who loves to bring awe, redemption, and delight. Loved. Seen. Safe.

The sound of stealthy prowling comes from the edge of the pond as a night hunter shifts and waits for dinner. Circle of life.

Moving along as the chill ever deepens, the hooting of an owl adds to the frosty night noises—haunting and lovely, it is primitive and wild.

The path around the pond circles back on itself, and my boots head back to the cabin. Thoughts of the cheerful fire in the firepit on the deck and the warm sherpa blanket urge me onward at a brisker pace.

Wrapped in the cozy blanket, Irish coffee in the large Christmas mug warms my cold hands, steam rising merrily as the fire mesmerizes me.

A scrabbling, crunchy noise interrupts my reveries as a creature moves about to the left of the deck, digging through pine needles and foliage for a midnight snack. Curious glowing eyes spy on me. The shadowy outline of a fat raccoon in the faint reach of the firelight watches me until her curiosity wanes, and she moves along.

Leaning back in the deck chair, the stars appear strewn about like so much glitter landing at random points. But nothing is truly random. The night sky is beautifully planned and decorated with patterns and puzzles of light created to lead the ancient traveler.

Frosty breath wafts up as if making its way to the austere

moon that guides, watches, and travels the night sky. Fascinating to imagine all the eyes that have looked up in the night for navigation and a sense of constancy in a world that doesn't always seem that way. A balm to lonely souls, the shining beacon of light makes things feel safer and less chaotic.

The shepherds on that holy and silent night looked up into the same chilled, star-filled sky that I see on my deck as the fire glows and snickers to itself. The same moon watched on as the Holy One became man, as angelic hosts filled the still and starry night with the most awe-inspiring, stunning display of power and love that humankind has ever known.

It is not by happenstance that eyes are drawn upward—seeking wisdom, direction, meaning, safety, love, and blessed peace.

From a cold and silent winter night, filled with moonlight and stars, came the Light of the world. A Divine exchange between Creator and creation. Ultimate gift. Unconditional love. Emmanuel.

Warm bed beckons, and I head inside, mind full of awe as I struggle to comprehend the enormity of the gift humanity was given on that night so long ago.

The old wood stove burns quiet, drowsy warmth. I curl up under quilts and comforters as the light of the moon gently glows through the snug window. Thoughts of angels, joy, and eternity soothe and calm into a restful sleep—a silent and holy night where all is calm and bright under a December moon.

# Mary, Did You Know?

Mary, the mother of Jesus. She is one of my favorite women in the Bible. I aspire to have her spirit—the way she watches, listens, and fully takes in the miracles she witnesses. The miraculous becomes her life and collides with her humble and ordinary humanity. Her life story literally alters history, bringing saving hope to mankind.

I imagine her thoughts, wonder, fear, and acceptance as the angel Gabriel appears to her and says, "Greetings, you who are highly favored! The Lord is with you!"[1] It captivates me! What was it like to have been her?

Did Mary wonder what Gabriel meant when he said she was highly favored? Did it terrify her that God looked upon her and trusted her, a virgin from a tiny town, to give birth to the Savior of the world? "He will be great and will be called the Son of the Most High, who will be given the throne of his father David,

---

1   Luke 1:28

who will reign over the house of Jacob forever."[2] She would be the mother of the One whose kingdom will never end. How can this be? Yet she believed that "…nothing is impossible with God."[3] She received this honor and said, "I am the Lord's servant, may it be to me as you have said."[4]

I am not asked to birth a Savior, but I am asked to seek Him and love Him with all my heart, mind, and spirit. I may not be visited by an angel of the Most High God and given a commission that will alter history, but I am asked to boldly tell my story.

What were Mary's thoughts as she and Joseph set out on the long and wearying journey to Bethlehem? Did she worry about how they would get there with her being so far with child? Did Mary contemplate the enormity of what was set before her? Was she cold? Did she wish God had chosen someone else? Yet, they were obedient. They trusted God. I like to believe that the supernatural sound of Gabriel's voice, his greeting and encouragement to her, and the awe of the blessing bestowed upon her played over and over in her mind as the God of all creation comforted her and reminded her that nothing is impossible.

As she wrapped her newborn son in cloths and gently placed Him in the manger with the sounds of the animals settling in for the night, I imagine Mary listening to the rejoicing of heaven as the heavenly hosts praised God and sang of His glory and the newly born Peace and Hope of mankind. What was it like knowing that this was happening because of the birth of her first-born son? The very words of Gabriel coming to pass as prophecy

2   Luke 1:32-33
3   Luke 1:37
4   Luke 1:38

was fulfilled in her hearing, watching, and listening as angels sang and rejoiced. This would be what Mary treasured and stored up in her heart. I can see her gentle smile as she reflected on all that had been spoken and prophesied over her and her baby boy. Jesus, the Son of God, the Prince of Peace, Mighty Warrior, the Savior of mankind.

Did Mary feel wonder and awe? Was her heart full of hope, joy, love, and anticipation? As she looked at Him, new, small, and fragile, did her heart fill to the brim with love and expectation? Did she comprehend that this precious baby boy would be her deliverer? That her firstborn son would die for her sins. I wonder if her spirit discerned that this baby would cause her such joy and such deep sorrow.

Mary could not have foreseen all that her son would mean to me—an ordinary, imperfect, fanciful woman, 2000 years in the future. She couldn't know all that I ponder and store up in my heart about what He has done, will do, and is doing. How I know He dances, rejoices, and sings over me; how prophesy flows from His mouth as He calls me Daughter and speaks to all that is not, as though it was, and it becomes what He pleases. All the small moments and miracles known only to my soul that I store up as my treasure; all the revelation, healing, and protection He has showered on me—things that my soul and spirit cannot comprehend. It is all undeserved but given with such a wildly, fiercely generous love. Mary, did you know?

"But Mary treasured up all these things and pondered them in her heart."[5]

5   Luke 2:19

# Winter Village

A CRESCENT RAY of filtered sunlight peeps in through the upstairs bedroom window.

Languid, lazy stretches; it's cozy under the heavy heirloom quilt. I doze a bit longer, enjoying the peace and quiet, until the calico cat frisks and pounces on my moving foot, forcing me to get up and begin the day.

Soft, fluffy slipper socks wait next to the pine wood nightstand. Quilt-warmed feet are toasty padding down the narrow stairs; the familiar creak at the fifth step from the bottom is comforting.

Snow!

A light snow has fallen in the night, coating the garden and the stone fence with a sparkly spunkiness that beckons a walk to the village.

But first, coffee!

The warm, comforting coffee scent permeates the chilly kitchen. Crispy bacon on toast sounds delicious this snow-bright morning—just enough until I make my way to Penny's Pastries in the village square.

The watery sunlight filtering through the slowly building clouds begs for knee-high snow boots, the puffed navy-blue snow jacket and thick, red tartan scarf, navy gloves, and a beanie. Festive and snug!

The fluffy white cat lounges in his cardboard box bed on the end of the couch, watching sleepily as I don my winter apparel. He is quite happy to lie about for the morning, nestled down on the red fleece blanket tucked into the box.

Wrapped up and warm, I venture into the pretty snow-covered garden and out the creaky, wooden gate to begin my snowy adventure.

More snow than I realize has fallen during the night. The way it gently drifts and pillows the lane into the village square is lovely and inviting—that satisfying snow-crunch underfoot.

Winking, colorful Christmas lights add a festive sparkle to the windows of Della's Curio Shoppe on the corner. Antique Christmas decorations and assorted glass bowls filled with hard candies invite one to step inside and browse the eclectic trinkets. A calming scent of vanilla, fir, and old things tease the senses. A jolly-looking antique snowman catches my eye. Carefully wrapped trinket in hand, I venture on into the village.

The small group of well-bundled carolers gracing the entrance to the old stone church sing with gusto as they nod a greeting to those who stop to listen. Their blending sopranos and altos swirl up and away into the wintry air on frosted breath. A wistful sigh of nostalgia brushes against me as I remember Christmases past with caroling, hot cocoa, and festive holiday laughter…the anticipation of Christmas Eve and the Greatest gift to mankind.

Ah! Penny's Pastries!

The scent of baking, heady and delicious, wafts from the wreathed door as patrons come and go, leaving a path in the powdery snow. Will she have fresh cream currant scones? She does! I settle myself, the scone, and some steamy Winter Blend tea at a rustic table near the windows. People watching!

Across the square, Nadia's Toys & Treasures is doing brisk business this morning! The festive window display draws in the strolling families as they watch the model train set navigate the miniature hills and tunnels covered in flakey snow. Tiny sheep and cattle settled on the snowy fields watch its progress. Wide-eyed children beg to go in and see where that tiny train goes on its round-and-round journey. Adventure!

Kitty-corner is Bea's Nifty Notions n' Such, serving the sew-ers, knitters, and crafters of the village. Brightly colored holiday ribbons, soft knit hats, mittens, and a plump Mrs. Claus at an antique sewing machine, adorn her display windows. It reminds me of my mother and grandmother—their beautiful handmade gifts and crafts so lovingly created. Two older ladies with bright purple hats and matching scarves bustle out the door. The holiday-themed bags are filled with supplies for their next sewing project.

The clock-tower bells chime the hour with a deep, silvery gong. How time flies! There is more to see, so I head out into the bustling square.

Lunchtime!

Next stop, Lazzaro's Deli. A prosciutto, ham, and Swiss cheese sandwich with a few swipes of golden mustard, thin-sliced red onion, a splash of balsamic and olive oil, just a touch, mind, and some plump grapes accompany me on a hike up the hill behind the village. There is a small grove of pines at the top where adventurous children haul their sleds and all varieties of hand-made sliding contraptions to fly down the slope—yelping, shouting, and having a splendid time. Freedom and flight!

Weathered pine picnic tables are scattered around the grove for year-round picnickers, each table with a view of the sledders and village below. What a pleasant way to spend the afternoon. Memories pop up of climbing the hill at night with thermoses of hot cocoa and Baileys to look at the village adorned in Christmas lights. Spellbinding!

A quick brindle dog and large German Shepherd dash through the grove, pouncing and digging in the snow in search of the ball they have been fetching. While the dogs are busy, their owners pull out their picnic, hoping to get in a few bites before the ball is found. The dog-kicked and flung snow comes dangerously close to my table. Laughing, I take that as my signal to head back down the hill.

Crisp, pine-scented, wintry air tousles my hair, peeping out from under the beanie. Filling my lungs with the cold air is so invigorating! I'm alive and well on this wonderful day.

At the edge of the village, I change course and walk the lesser traveled side lanes. The snow drifts are deeper here but still navigable. The sun begins an early descent in the mountains, and the shadows grow longer. The fading, muted light is a bit eerie as clouds move in and hover lower in the winter sky. An unmistakable feeling of snow.

The quaint and tumbled houses are pretty with their covers of snow and puffing chimneys. Safe and homey. A group of children jostle out one of the doors and into the nearby field, pummeling each other with snowballs. Shouts and whoops of laughter break up the quiet.

Heading to the left, I follow the lane running along the banks of a stream. It passes from the hills through the village and out and beyond. Normally noisy and full of life, the quietening of winter renders it silent and still, as if in a deep and restful sleep. As I cross the sturdy stonework bridge spanning the iced-over stream, it broadens out into a wide, gentle lake frozen into the perfect ice-skating rink. Ordering a large hot cocoa from the festive concessions stand, I grab a seat on one of the nearby benches.

Dinnertime!

The Aberdeen Café and Mama's Diner fill up with hungry shoppers and families who need a quick refuel and rest before ice skating begins. I'm happy I have half a sandwich left over from lunch. Trekking up and down the hill made me hungry. As the heat from the hot cocoa leaches into my chilly hands, I gaze around the square at the beautifully lit fir tree with its merry winking lights and lovely lit-up angel at the top. I imagine a dark starry night long ago when angels' songs announced the arrival of Hope.

With dinner finished, the brave and adventurous head out onto the ice. They are all in top form! Some glide by with calm, happy smiles, while others slip along with mouths formed into a nervous O as they precariously zip and zing across the ice. There will be more than a few sore bums and knees before the night is over.

The village is festive and welcoming with its lovely lights and lit greenery. I hesitate to head home yet, but it's been a long day. The coziness of my aunt and uncle's cottage, with the crackling fire they will have blazing, beckons me to go on home.

Finishing the hot cocoa, I take another look at the cheerful shops and happy skaters. What a lovely day!

I scoop up my package from the curio shop and make my way along the darkening lane to the cottage. As I walk and breathe in the frigid night air, gentle snow begins to fall on the winter village. The large fluffy flakes are soft and gentle. So peaceful. I marvel at the way they flutter and float on the wintry night air, each going their own way. There is a deliberateness to the random way they descend and find their landing place. Each one with a specific spot that adds to the piling snow drifts—each one needed. I imagine the Creator's joy and excitement as each one is uniquely crafted and thought out. Humanity isn't so different from these beautiful snowflakes.

Turning onto Lakeview Lane, I pause to take in the cottage before heading inside. So lovely, the way it sparkles and winks, white lights outlining its edges and curves, smoke gently chuffing from the stone chimney. Inviting. Lovely memories of my day in the village are safely tucked away as snowy peace descends on the winter village.

...with the Father

# Prayer

THE INTERSECTION of the Divine and humanity. Awe-inspiring. It's hard to wrap the mind around this mystery of supernatural communion with the Creator. The One who formed us, named us, called us out from nothing into what is, and prophesied over us what will be. Extraordinary, beautiful, mysterious.

It is the God-breathed breath in our lungs transforming into words whispered, shouted, sobbed, laughed, and somehow ascending, floating, soaring up, up into the very presence of the One who formed the stars and called the Earth into being. Into the Holy of Holies, in the presence of angels and cherubim, our words thought and spoken, know exactly where to go as they search out the ear and heart of the Father. Our words and every thought know they will be found when they seek His attention. A magnetism that draws our need, praise, and sometimes our fury and rage straight to Him. Undivided attention amid billions of voices. How is that possible?

Yet it is. The meticulous attention, time, and precision with which we were each formed allow us direct access to the One who knows us best. Nothing is hidden from Him. The raw vulnerability of that exposure is terrifying and unsettling, yet I find safety and rest here. No disguise, mask, or self-righteous posturing happens in His presence. Flowery words and Christianese have no place in honest, raw, desperate conversations with the One who knows our every breath and move, the One who has our names engraved on the palms of His scarred hands.

There are times when the wounds and need are so raw and deep that no adequate words exist to speak it out, yet the Spirit knows—the pain, the rage, the gnawing, indescribable need that cries for release. He is right there in the middle of it, interceding "for us with groans too deep for words."[1] Love. Comfort. Safety.

At times the joy, victory, and delight are too overwhelming to express, and His Spirit births in us deep, healing laughter and tears that could never be expressed with mere words. How He loves us, how intimately He knows us. How He delights in supernatural conversation with us!

It isn't hard talking to Him. Open your mouth and allow your mind and your spirit to connect with Him. You are never less than or too much. You are enough. You are just right. He does hear you. Jesus wants to heal you and offer you hope, peace, joy, and strength to get through all that life tosses out. He's a best Friend, Father, Healer, Comforter, Warrior, the Prince of Peace, and you have His complete and undivided attention. So, grab your favorite mug, fill it with something soothing, lovely, and warm, and have a chat with your Father…with or without words.

---

1   Romans 8:26

# Longing

RISING UP from deep in my soul is a sensation that is difficult to describe, but I need to name it. Somehow that will make it feel safe and predictable, possibly even controllable. It is pressure that builds and needs a release, a cry that can only be satisfied by an answering calm, a gentling of the urgency, by a whispered word, saying, "Peace, be still child; how very close I am to you."

It is birthed in quiet moments of meditation and worship where time ceases to exist, as I have Your undivided attention. My voice and Your Spirit mix and intertwine in the Heavenlies bringing delight to Your heart and setting into motion things I could never comprehend. It is so beautiful, yet not safe and certainly not predictable. It surges up as I fall to my knees in awe of all that You are, knowing that the small bit I do know of You is almost more than I can bear. Knowing there is more, that You are richer and more brilliant than my most vivid dreams, frightens me. It is not safe or predictable and cannot be contained. No—it is holy, a consuming fire, pure, wild, and more fierce and passionate than I can handle on my own.

It swells up when my fingers finally release their death grip on what I knew all along I could never control yet almost died in trying. I hear it in the sound of chains falling and walls crumbling as another stronghold tumbles to the ground, the scent of victory overcoming the stench of defeat. The feeling comes as a wave, a pounding of the heart as Your anointing falls when obedience calls and is answered with, "Yes, Lord, here I am."

It is there when the howling loneliness shouts for filling and claws in desperation until Your presence is given permission and enfolds and permeates the void. I sense it when unspeakable joy and peace that passes all understanding snaps like a banner in the wind, high above the circumstances and distractions of life, proclaiming that Jehovah Nissi is my covering and victory.

In Your presence, I understand the sensation is a soul-deep desire for You—a needy emptiness that can only be filled by all that You are. It is the craving my spirit knows will only be satisfied when I am forever in Your presence, an obsession keeping me hungry and thirsty for revelation, wisdom, truth, and a startling intimacy found only with You. It isn't safe or predictable, certainly not controllable, and will be with me until I see You face to face.

So, I will let go and embrace the wild fierceness of it. I will welcome it with open arms and a tender heart. I will name it longing.

# Tattoos and Driftwood

A BRISK WIND snaps and fluffs tendrils of auburn hair peeking out from under her olive-green beanie. It feels so invigorating as if the wind is beckoning her to come out and walk on the beach. Perhaps it knows something feels different this morning, like that feeling when an elusive word is on the tip of your tongue, but your brain won't quite let it go.

This beach is Misty's favorite place and has been since she discovered it several years ago, quite by accident, actually. After spending time with friends in Santa Cruz before one of them headed to a new job in Texas, Misty decided to take a little detour on her way home just to see what she might see. Rounding a curve, there it was, laid out before her in all its glory! A lovely beach cove set off the road with a sandy little parking lot to accommodate visitors.

Misty pulled off, parked her yellow VW Bug, and that was it—she was in love with this beach.

Lately, life has been hard and confusing, complicated, and draining. The life path she dreamed of is not panning out, and it weighs heavily on her heart. Patience is not her bent, and the desire to move things along is a constant battle in her weary mind. Shouldn't she be there by now? Why wasn't she finding her niche?

Full of hope for a day of clearing her mind, she steps onto the sand into the wind and salty smell of the sea. Deep cleansing breaths, she tells herself. Deep, long, and cleansing. The vibrancy of the water holds anticipation in the micro sparkles she sees dancing on the swell of each wave. Heeding the call, she gingerly hops into the foamy sea and catches her breath at the cold, crisp tingle on her bare feet. The dramatic inhale of breath feels lovely and empowering. It feels comforting. Some of the fear and worry escape on the exhale. Is that a lightness in her soul?

"What do I do now?" she asks the sea, willing it to part with its ancient wisdom.

Walking along the wet sand, she alternately runs toward and dodges the ever-coming waves. For the first time in a while, she is having fun!

Up ahead, she sees something in the sand just out of reach of the waves. How odd, she thinks. What is it? It appears to be a small pile of driftwood. Ever curious, Misty investigates and discovers someone has spelled out the word JOY with the driftwood. It is gnarled and holey with striations of dark and light in the sea-soaked wood. Pausing to look at the driftwood, she feels what might be joy. Her mouth relaxes into a gentle smile, which, if she is honest with herself, has not happened in a while. Well, not a genuine smile. Hmmm. Joy. Yes, she does feel it. It's been simmering there just below the surface, blocked by worry, fear, and feeling left behind while others are off making their mark. Feeling like she doesn't measure up.

Continuing down the beach, soaking in the joy and letting it do its thing, she detects a lightness in her step and her shoulders relaxing. The sweet sun pours warmth into her bones, yet not the overwhelming heat that makes one run for the shade. Stopping to scan the sea and sand behind her, Misty sees her footprints. They look purposeful and confident like these prints have a destination in mind and are confidently heading there. The sea edges closer to her footprints and will soon wash them away as if they never existed. The past being taken and what is before her opening wide.

There are not many beachcombers out this morning. Mid-week keeps the crowds away, and Misty likes that. Up ahead, she hears barking and yipping from a sleek, brindle dog dancing with delight over the stick about to be tossed into the shallow waves. Being a dog lover, Misty briskly walks toward the middle-aged woman tossing the stick. She notices black yoga pants pushed up near the woman's knees to keep from getting soaked, a camo--colored hoodie with rolled-up sleeves, and short, fluffed light brown hair that dances and tosses in the crisp sea wind.

Smiling as she approaches, the woman waves, calls out a greeting, and tosses the stick high at the same time. As the wet dog returns with the stick, the woman reaches down to stroke its sleek body and gets a sandy, toothy grin. He wants her to hurry and throw the stick again. "He will do this all day, you know," the woman laughs. "This is our happy place."

As they exchange small talk and watch the escapades of the dog, Misty notices the woman has tattoos on her arms. One says Be Still and another Faith over Fear. She is surprised how these simple words tattooed on a stranger fill her with such emotion—this is what her tired heart and dry soul need. How she longs to just be still and let go of the fear that cripples her; fear of the unknown, that she isn't making a difference, and the constant striving that saps her energy.

Shyly, she asks the woman, "May I ask about your tattoos? This sounds weird, but I am drawn to them. I think they're speaking to me."

"Of course!" the woman replies. "These tattoos have special meaning. I've been through some rough patches, things I thought would break me. They remind me of all I have weathered, so I had them etched in a place I could revisit anytime."

As the silence spins out, the woman turns to look at her, forest-green eyes compassionate and knowing, holding Misty's gaze for a moment. "I don't know what's weighing on you, honey, but I believe everything happens for a reason. We all have a specific purpose on Earth, and sometimes to find it, we need to be still and let it come to us. Joy will come if you let it."

As the woman speaks, Misty feels peace flow over her back and neck. She has a more confident tilt to her chin and senses a shift in the atmosphere as she embraces letting go.

"Thank you," Misty replies. "I know why I needed to be here this morning."

As she moves down the beach and circles back at the cliff with the purple flowers, Misty's parched soul feels softer, and her insides are less strung up with anxiety. What if all she needs to do for now is be still? What if there is a Creator who has plans and a specific purpose just for her? Walking toward the car, the small smile on her face is brighter. She feels joy and delight at the beautiful beach, the warm sun, and the constant reassuring shushing of the sea.

After a few more hefty tosses of the stick, it's time to head home. The dog drops the stick, and the woman smiles and offers up a silent prayer of thanks. This random, yet not, encounter on the beach blessed her, too.

Gathering up her coffee thermos, the wet dog, and the precious fetching stick, the woman in the camo hoodie understands why she felt such a pull to the sea and this specific beach today. Tattoos and JOY written in driftwood. The still, small voice isn't wrong, and what blessings come from heeding it.

# Anniversary

THIS SIMPLE WORD holds a lot of meaning. Its definition is "the date on which an event took place in a previous year." It doesn't say this event was particularly good, bad, or otherwise, but it represents something significant, something that is seared in the memory with long-reaching effects on life going forward. Marriage is an event that typically comes to mind, along with birthdates, the first day of school, graduation, and the death of a loved one.

For me, the Thanksgiving season is the anniversary of an event that was completely unwelcome, blindsiding, and heartbreaking. On November 23rd, 2010, my doctor told my husband and me that I had breast cancer. It was the day before Thanksgiving. I find that ironic. Thanksgiving, when we are supposed to count our blessings, be grateful, go around the beautifully decorated table, and list three things and people we are thankful for that year. It is supposed to be happy, restful, and full of laughter, blessings, and appreciation. That is not how we felt. It was a time of sadness, fear, helplessness, not knowing if I would be alive the following year, deep anger, and many emotions that I still do not have adequate words to describe. I was not thankful.

The next several years were full of chemo, radiation, Herceptin, anti-nausea, and various other meds pumped into me 24/7. There were prods, pokes, surgeries, and so many scans and tests, blood work, scares, and triumphs. And every year, the anniversary of one of the worst days of my life.

Yet…now that there is some distance from that first anniversary and the scares come less often, I find I am thankful. The scares and fears will always be with me. They are part of me now. What I learned through this experience and living through these anniversaries has taught me more about life and God's love, compassion, and mercy than anything else.

There are those who say to forget the past and all that it brings up and focus only on the good, the positive, and the present. I agree on a certain level. However, I don't believe in erasing those circumstances and events God allowed into our lives for a specific season and purpose. Nothing touches us that He doesn't first filter through His hands. Nothing. Life, death, pain, heartbreak, joy, and triumph. It all serves a purpose. I don't know how it will be used. I can't say it might not break our hearts, but I absolutely believe these things will be used for good. The imagery of God's hands filtering and sifting events, people, and circumstances that enter my life makes me feel safe, valuable, and protected. We are safe with Him. We can trust Him with ourselves.

I will not forget this anniversary. I will embrace it and allow the emotions attached to it to flow. Some memories don't hurt as much anymore because I see clearly how close Jesus was to me. This trauma brought me close to Him. It had to because I had nothing else to cling to and no other hope but in Him.

I don't know what your anniversaries are nor the impact they have had on your life and the lives of those you love, but I do know that God was there on that first anniversary. He is here right now. He saw you then, and He sees you now. You are not alone. He is working it all out. It may be hard and frightening or a wild ride filled with joy, victory, and new seasons, but in the midst of it all, there is hope, extravagant hope!

Psalm 119:114 "You are my refuge and my shield; your word is my source of hope."

Jeremiah 29:11 "For I know the plans I have for you," declares the Lord, "plans to prosper you and not to harm you, plans to give you hope and a future."

# Sanctuary

I SIT IN the sanctuary of my heart, still, waiting for You. I no longer fear what is in my heart nor try to deny it exists. You hold out Your hands to receive it—the damage, the sin, the struggles, the fear, the place where deep hurts and secrets dwell. You are not afraid. You smile as I hand them over, some quickly and with ease, others with hesitation, and still others that take time, as I painfully and deliberately choose to release them to You, one finger at a time, one muscle at a time. What You will do with these things of mine, I am not entirely sure, but I do know You want them. In Your mercy and love, You take them and transform all that I thought was lost, used up, and devastated beyond hope into a thing of rare and poignant beauty. It is so precious and sacred that Your Spirit hovers over Your redeemed and transformed work, nurturing it, breathing life, wisdom, and power over it, releasing authority and boldness into it, and forever changing me.

How can I be the same when Your holiness, grace, and sovereignty intercept me in my humanity, frailty, and poverty?

Not possible. To be in Your presence for but a moment leaves Your fragrance, Your taste, Your fingerprints everywhere! How could this not be my greatest desire? But…life, busyness, and superficiality also vie for my attention, and the battle is hard.

Yet, Your Spirit, which watches over the transformation, is constantly at work even if Your voice seems distant. You are still shouting Your delight over me, rejoicing above me, and dancing all around me. Will I choose to still my heart and mind long enough to hear You speak in the wind, feel Your touch in its caress, catch Your scent in the flowers, and dance before You with no shame? Will I be still long enough and choose to trust You enough to take my hidden hopes and treasured dreams and place them in Your outstretched hands? You placed them in my heart. You have given me visions, dreams, and desires too deep to name, yet You ask for them back. Yes, I will give them to You. For You are good, You are faithful, and You are truth. Only You can give wings to the plans You have for me. You say that "no eye has seen, no ear has heard, no mind has conceived what God has prepared for those who love Him."[2]

Because of Calvary, undeserved sacrifice, and mercy, because of love that freely flows from Your throne and pours into a scarred yet hopeful heart, I can sit here in peace and safety, calling my heart Your sanctuary. Thank You for the treasure You revealed in what was once a lonely and desolate place. Where the Spirit of the Lord is, there is freedom.

---

2   1 Corinthians 2:9

# Pruning

SUMMER is drawing to a close. The months of bright, festive flowers that beckon and sing to the pollinators and picnickers are dwindling down. There will be a few days of heated fury and defiance, where summer rebels just a bit—blazing hot and fierce. Time is almost up, and it knows.

The garden knows, too, and begins the descent into autumn. The spring and summer flowering plants and bushes slow and droop, dropping dried blooms, except for those that flourish and delight in autumn, bringing fresh color and excitement to a waning garden.

With this changing of the guard comes a season of pruning. Much needs to be done to keep the garden looking loved, cared for, and peaceful. Garden shears, trimmers, and trowels are still needed.

Upon close inspection, one sees the stems, leaves, vines, and small branches shut down, wither, and die back. The perennials need this season of pruning for survival; they need someone to cut away and remove those areas that are no longer serving them or the garden. At times the pruning seems brutal, harsh, and perhaps cruel, as some parts are cut away so severely that there is hardly any of the original plant left. All is cut away that is not actively helping, nurturing, and stimulating growth in the plant. Those dead and dying parts suck vital nutrients from the healthy stems, branches, and leaves. A good gardener knows that they cannot be left to compete with and deplete the healthy plant.

Bending close to check each branch and stem, the gardener determines where best to trim and cut away. At first glance, a stem or branch may look completely wasted away, yet a closer look reveals tiny, minute new growth attempting to push its way out. The gardener values this new growth, barely visible except to the one who actively seeks and delights in nourishing this fledgling sprout of new life. All that is above it will be removed and tossed away, allowing plenty of room and careful tending to encourage the new life.

Do you see how this imagery of a master gardener lovingly tending his or her garden applies so beautifully to how the Creator lovingly and intentionally prunes, tends, and cares for us?

The pruned plant may look bedraggled and worse for wear, hacked and shorn off, appearing vulnerable and fragile. But this is where the unseen work takes place in the root system below the surface. With the dead and decaying parts pruned away, the roots are free to prepare and strengthen the fragile plant for new life. The quiet season of strength-building is vital for this plant and for us, too. When the Master Gardener deems it is time, new life will burst up, break forth and take its place in the Garden of

Life, amid humanity, where the plant and you and I will live out our purpose, delight those meant to encounter us and be deeply nourished from a root system well established and fed by the Master Gardener and His living water.

The pruning season is hard. It hurts and can leave us feeling like there is nothing left of us but stumpy, stick-like nubs that are ugly, barren, and have no purpose. But we can't see with the eyes of the Master Gardener, who sees these shorn-off places as a thing of great beauty and Divine Purpose because He knows what's coming. He sees the pruned places for what they are; stealers of joy, the heavy weight of bad habits, bitterness and anger, idols we erected in a search for happiness, and greedy competitors that rob precious energy. I imagine Him smiling and laughing in anticipation of all that He is doing below the surface to the root system of our lives. Every nip, cut, snip, and prune holds tremendous value and purpose. So, can we endure for a little while, during the quiet autumn of the pruning season, to see the joy, delight, and surprise that will spring forth?

# Ascending

THE CREATOR watches as they ascend to the heavenlies. Lovely, iridescent conversations drift up from the souls of His creation. Gently capturing every spoken and unspoken request in His hand, He attends to them all with love and delight. Engraved on His palms are names, so many names, each one a special treasure with His undivided attention. He listens with deep compassion as the fragrance of our need for Him fills, swirls, and mingles with cherubim song and voices of the saints. A song that is deep, mysterious, and filled with prophecy pours from His mouth and flows down to bathe and hover over us. Deep calls to deep as He intervenes, commands, and performs the miraculous. His timing is perfect.

Each prayer, groan, praise, and cry rise upward on the delicate, life-giving vapors of His very breath breathed into our lungs. Returning to the Creator, they seek peace, protection, and healing; compassion, provision, and love—that deep need to be known and seen—to matter.

Never resting, omniscient, and omnipresent, the Almighty is aware of all that concerns His cherished ones. No need, thought, or desire is hidden from Him. The first fluttering open of an eyelid in the morning, the scent of pine being inhaled and enjoyed, the sting of rejection, and late-night tears from a broken heart are not lost on Him. Full of compassion and mercy, He sings over the pain, fear, joy, and mundane, speaking that which is not into existence and calling home those for whom eternity with Him is beckoning.

When a wound is so deep that the wounded one has no words yet cries out with groans and weeping, He is in the midst of it, speaking peace, speaking healing, speaking Himself into the chaos. It must quiet, obey and make space for His plan, healing, and comfort. Just a brush from the hem of His robe is enough to calm a soul in distress, heal the body, mind, and spirit, and quiet the voices of fear, worry, despair, and evil. His thoughts and His glance are always enough. Omnipotent.

When shouts of joy and words of thanksgiving tumble from grateful lips and eyes are tear-stained with joy and deliverance, He is there. He rejoices with the heavenly host over a prodigal coming home, a life healed, a relationship mended, a soul repentant and forgiven.

The prayers whispered in the mundane, unseen happenings of an ordinary day are revered and never overlooked. There is a specific purpose for each second granted to His child, and not one is trivial.

There is peace and safety in knowing that we are not anonymous. We are fully known and seen in a sea of humanity desperate for hope, peace, protection, and healing. Psalm 139:1-6 declares, "You have searched me, Lord, and you know me. You know when I sit and when I rise, you perceive my thoughts from afar. You discern my going out and my lying down; you are familiar with all my ways. Before a word is on my tongue, you, Lord, know it completely. You hem me in behind and before, and you lay your hand upon me. Such knowledge is too wonderful for me, too lofty for me to attain."

The prayers of creation will never cease ascending to the Father's ears. He will forever receive them with love and mercy, giving grace, undivided attention, and care to each one. Billions of soul-whispers and cries continuously flow upward. Yours will never be lost in the crowd. You will never be irrelevant and unseen. Your voice will always be a beautiful incense perfuming the Throne Room of the Most High. You are not anonymous to the One who loves you best.

# Voices

It's ONLY a little sidestep off the path, a tiny compromise. My body and soul are tired. The road ahead looks lonely and slow going. I feel anxious, stuck, and irritable. I have dreams and plans! I am impatient to move forward at a much faster pace than this narrow, less-traveled road will allow. I heard You when You said You have beautiful plans for me and that You are my Shepherd. I heard You when You said You'll guide me along the right paths for Your name's sake and for my good...I heard You. But...I am certain this new path I discovered, veering off to the left, will get me there much faster.

I'm moving at a good, brisk pace along my new path, feeling accomplished and determined. I stop for a rest when I notice a storm brewing on the horizon. A feeling of unease begins to slither along my back and around my shoulders. My legs feel heavy, weighed down, and sluggish. The slight breeze is picking up, and the air has a frightening intensity that builds and hovers. The light breeze becomes a stronger gust and a howling wind that scours and rages. The storm is here. The rain pelts, stings, and bruises.

My protective armor of misunderstood self-reliance is violently shorn away as Rebellion is brought low. There is nothing left of the well-insulated life that I padded with denial, supported with beams of pride, and girded up with planks of lukewarm complacency. The storm took my painstakingly fretted-over structure and swept it away. I think I always knew it would. But self-reliance is addicting. Rebellion masks itself as a unique strength of character ushering in pride and arrogance and an entitled sense of self-righteousness. I feel the vulnerability of having nothing to cling to as I sit in deep silence. It is deafening.

"What do I have left?" I softly cry. You have removed everything in one fell swoop. I sit in the barren ruins of what used to be, of the things, accolades, and accomplishments I thought I earned from all my hard work, control, and endless striving. Wasn't I entitled to it?

Silence.

"Where are You? Where were You when I made these poor choices? Why weren't You shouting for me to stop, change direction and wait? Why were You silent?

Silence.

"Do I even matter?" I whisper.

"Yes."

Was that Your voice breaking the silence? I've grown accustomed to my voice and the other voices that knew where the harder, less traveled path would lead me and were deeply afraid

I might choose it. How hard they worked to seduce me with visions of recognition, accomplishment, and worth! Self-reliance, Idolatry, and Pride merrily hissed and whispered in my ear exactly what I wanted to hear. Their voices slyly drowned out the one Voice I so desperately needed. Yours.

In the silence of the storm's aftermath, Your whispered words reverberate in the stillness. "I am Your Shepherd, and you lack nothing...I lead you beside quiet waters and give you rest; I refresh your soul and guide you along the right paths..."

I remember the other path I refused to take. There were boulders and some steep, narrow parts that looked daunting and difficult. It looked too hard, and I was tired. The peaceful easiness of the wide, comfortable path required little but cost a lot...only a tiny compromise, I thought...

The sly smiles of Rebellion, Idolatry, and Arrogance beckoned me, and I hurried to them. I turned away from You and headed along the wide path despite the little frissons of cold uneasiness that crept along my spine. I didn't want You there and my choices numbed Your voice into a breathy Whisper—barely discernable, but there. I was deceived and had no idea how to find You. Hopelessness sighed that it was too late, that You would be disappointed. Fear declared it would be too hard to go back—that I was lost and would never find my way.

"What now, Father?"

"Follow My voice."

Just beyond the storm wreckage, I see a small clearing. I clamber over strewn debris, broken idols, and some ruts and gouges in the ground. It is bright here. The air is fresh. Floating feathers—this is Holy ground. There is a deep pool in the clearing fed by a bubbling stream. I walk to the edge and am dismayed by my reflection. I'm dirty. I'm covered in debris and mud. My hair is tangled up with sticks and things I've collected along the way. I turn to You, and Your eyes pierce my soul and spirit, exposing my innermost thoughts. Instead of wounding, this exposure begins healing and restoring all that was lost and taken from me as I sidestepped Your plans and veered off course.

You gently nod Your head and gesture toward the clear pool. The water looks refreshing and inviting! Cool and pure. Am I brave enough to step in? The stench of all I have believed and rejected, attempted, and failed is overwhelming. I want to live again, and I dive in!

Here is mercy, deep love, and compassion. Here is healing, rejuvenation, and new life. I am fully known and accepted. The striving, searching, and fear are washed away. I hear singing and prophesy. I hear joy. I hear Your voice clearly. You tell me I am enough.

"Therefore, if anyone is in Christ, the new creation has come: The old has gone, the new is here!"[1]

---

1   2 Corinthians 5:17

# Acknowledgements

This book has been so much fun to write!

I continue to be thankful, surprised, and honored that God opened doors and made a way for me to write this second book. From His heart to my pen…

There are so many people that need a special thanks for helping Divine Appointments… get out in the world.

To…

My parents and family for always believing in me and spurring me on. You mean the world to me.

Tina Harrell and Wendy Moon for your genuine feedback, faithful friendship and prayers over me and all aspects of Divine Appointments… as it evolved into what God desired. You are blessings!

Jainell Gaitan, Kathryn Dunn and Heather Greaves for your friendship and invaluable and honest feedback on wording and design ideas. Your fresh eyes and thoughtful suggestions made this process smoother. You are treasures!

Kellie, Megan, Sherri, Archna, Ann, Mary, Alyssa, R and Kimberly. Writing this book while transitioning to military Mom life was not an easy feat. You all have been encouraging and helpful in finding the humor and beauty in this new season of life as well as your insightful feedback. You are brave and courageous women that I'm honored to call friends.

The lovely and talented women who transform my rough drafts into books I am proud to send off into the world. Pia Edberg for editing and sharpening up my words and thoughts so the voice of my book is heard, Jessie Cunniffe for bringing those words together into a beautiful blurb that fascinates and captures the attention, and Karolina Wudniak for taking the themes and message and creating the illustrations and cover designs that perfectly capture the soul and essence of my books.

I am grateful to each one of you!

# Author bio

Melissa Giomi, author of *Divine Encounters...* and *Divine Appointments...* is a Northern California native born in Redding. She lives in California with her husband and their pets. They have two adult children.

Melissa is passionate about Jesus, nature, books, and good coffee. She can be found puttering in the garden and enjoying nature's early morning antics on the patio. Melissa and her husband enjoy relaxing by the ocean or in the mountains, hiking, and camping in the Redwoods.

While seeking joy, hope, and healing on her journey through breast cancer and life's many seasons, Melissa discovered that divine appointments pop up in ordinary days and extraordinary circumstances. All it requires are eyes, hearts, and souls to be open to the Creator's invitation.